PIERS ANTHONY

STARMONT READER'S GUIDE 20

MICHAEL R. COLLINGS

Series Editor: Roger C. Schlobin

☆ **Starmont House** ☆
Mercer Island, Washington
1983

R0149710309
HUM

For Judi, with appreciation.

Library of Congress Cataloging in Publication Data:

Collings, Michael R.
  Piers Anthony.

  (Starmont reader's guide ; 20)
  Includes bibliographies and index.
  1. Anthony, Piers—Criticism and interpretation.
I. Title. II. Series.
PS3551.N73Z6 1983   813'.54   83-2466
ISBN 0-916732-53-3
ISBN 0-916732-52-5 (pbk.)

Copyright © 1983 by Starmont House.
All rights reserved. International copyrights reserved in all countries.
No part of this book may be reproduced in any form, except for brief
passages quoted in reviews, without expressed written consent of the
publisher.

Published by Starmont House, P.O. Box 851, Mercer Island, WA 98040,
USA. Composition by The Borgo Press. Cover design by Stephen
E. Fabian.

First Edition———November, 1983

DR. MICHAEL R. COLLINGS, currently Associate Professor of English
in the Communication Division at Pepperdine University, Malibu, also
edits *The Lamp-Post* of the Southern California C. S. Lewis Society.
His work on science fiction and fantasy includes papers and articles on
C. S. Lewis, Piers Anthony, Frank Herbert, Ursula K. Le Guin, and
genre and language in science fiction. He has published a volume of
poetry, short stories, and reviews, and co-authored a cookbook.

CONTENTS

ABBREVIATIONS

BC   *Battle Circle* (includes *Sos the Rope*, *Var the Stick*, *Neq the Sword*)

C   *Cluster*

CH   *Chthon*

CL   *Chaining the Lady*

CR   *Castle Roogna*

FT   *Faith of Tarot*

GT   *God of Tarot*

KQ   *Kirlian Quest*

MAC   *Macroscope*

NEQ   *Neq the Sword*

SC   *A Spell for Chameleon*

SOS   *Sos the Rope*

SM   *The Source of Magic*

VT   *Vision of Tarot*

I

CANON AND CHRONOLOGY

1934   Born Piers Anthony Dillingham Jacob; August 6, in Oxford, England.

1939   The Jacob family moves to Spain. His father, Alfred Jacob, was the head of the American Friends Service Committee (the international activity arm of the Quakers). During the family's stay in Spain, Alfred Jacob disappeared; he later smuggled a note out of prison informing his wife of his location. He was finally released and ordered to leave the country.

1940   The Jacob family moves to America.

1947   ". . . I discovered *Astounding SF* magazine at the age of 13. . . ." [1]

1954   First serious science-fiction writing.

1956   B.A., Goddard College, Vermont; *The Unstilled World* submitted as his thesis (a section of which was later reworked and published as *Sos the Rope*). Marries Carol Marble, June 25.

1957   Drafted into the Army in March; serves basic training at Fort Dix, survey training at Fort Sill, Oklahoma.

1959   Moves to Florida, his permanent residence.

1959-62 Works as technical writer, Electronics Communications, Inc., St. Petersburg, Florida.

1962   First short story sale; begins serious career as free-lance writer.

1963   Publishes "Possible to Rue," "Quinquepedalian."

1964   Publishes "Sheol" (with H. James Hotaling), "Encounter," Receives Teachers Certificate, University of Southern Florida.

1965   Publishes "Phog"; *Chthon* completed after seven years of writing. Teaches English for one year at Admiral Farragut Academy, St. Petersburg, Florida.

1966   Publishes "Mandroid" (with Robert E. Margroff and Andrew J. Offutt), "The Message" (with Frances Hall),

"The Ghost Galaxies," and "Payoff" (with Margroff). Receives Nebula nomination for "The Message." Resumes free-lance career, sells his first novel, *Chthon*. Attends Milford Session in Pennsylvania.

1967   Publishes *Chthon*, "Within the Cloud," "In the Jaws of Danger," "Prostho Plus," "Beak by Beak." Receives $5000 award for *Sos the Rope* in the *Fantasy & Science Fiction*/Pyramid Press/Kent Productions contest. Receives Nebula nomination for *Chthon*; completes *Omnivore* (second novel sale) and *The Ring*. Enters into serious contract conflicts with Ballantine. His first daughter, Penelope, born: "I regard the birth of my first child as the most signicant change in my life, ever." [2]

1968   Publishes *Omnivore*, *Sos the Rope*, *The Ring* (with Margroff); "The Alien Rulers," "Getting Through University." Receives Hugo nomination for *Chthon*.

1969   Publishes *Macroscope*; "The Life of the Stripe," "None But I," "Alf Laylah Wa Laylah" (non-fiction), and "Hasan (Part I)." Receives Hugo nomination for "Getting Through University."

1970   Publishes *The E.S.P. Worm* (with Margroff); "Small Mouth, Bad Taste," "The Whole Truth," "The Bridge," "Hasan (Part II)," "Equals Four," "Orn," "Wood You?," "Monarch," and "Hearts." Receives Hugo nominations for *Macroscope* and as Best Fan Writer, Nebula nomination for "The Bridge." His second daughter, Cheryl, born.

1971   Publishes *Prostho Plus*, *Orn*.

1972   Publishes *Var the Stick*; "In the Barn," "Up Schist Creek," "Hard Sell," "Black Baby," "Hurdle." Receives Nebula nomination for "In the Barn." Diagnosed as diabetic, which results in the non-fiction *Death or Dialysis*, with Lawrence Kahana.

1973   Publishes *Race Against Time*; articles on various topics for St. Petersburg *Times*.

1974   Publishes *The Bamboo Bloodbath*, *Kiai!*, *Mistress of Death*, "Ki" (with Roberto Fuentes), *Rings of Ice*, *Triple Detente*, and an article on school for disabled children in the St. Petersburg *Times*.

1975   Publishes *Phthor*, *Neq the Sword*, *Ninja's Revenge* (with Fuentes), "Kiai—How it Began."

1976   Publishes *Amazon Slaughter* (with Fuentes), *But What of Earth?* (a disputed "collaboration" with Robert Coulson), *OX*, *Steppe*, "Three Misses."

1977   Publishes *Cluster*, *A Spell for Chameleon*. Receives the August Derleth Fantasy Award for best novel for *A Spell for Chameleon*.

1978   Publishes *Battle Circle* (a combined edition of *Sos the Rope*,

Var the Stick, Neq the Sword), *Chaining the Lady, Kirlian Quest.* Receives Hugo nomination for best book-length fantasy, *A Spell for Chameleon*.

1979   Publishes *Castle Roogna, God of Tarot, Pretender* (with Frances Hall), *The Source of Magic*.

1980   Publishes *Faith of Tarot, Vision of Tarot, Split Infinity, Thousandstar*.

1981   Publishes *Blue Adept, Mutes*; "On The Uses of Torture."

1982   Publishes *Centaur Aisle, Juxtaposition*, and *Viscous Circle. Ogre, Ogre* published September 1982.

1983   Publishes *Night Mare*.

Works in Progress: *On a Pale Horse; Ogam Palimpsest; Volk*

NOTES:

1. Cliff Biggers, "An Interview with Piers Anthony," *Science Fiction Review*, November 1977, p. 57 [rpt. from *Future Retrospective*.]
2. Biggers, p. 59.

II

INTRODUCTION

Piers Anthony Dillingham Jacob, better known as Piers Anthony, sold his first science-fiction story in 1962 and his first novel four years later. Since then, he has become one of the most prolific and controversial writers in the genre. In the fourteen years since *Chthon* was sold, he has published over forty novels, among them science-fictional treatments of the Tarot, astrology, Kirlian auras, and even a quest for the identity of God. His fantasies are characteristically exuberant and lively, often incorporating elements of Arabian mythic patterns. His Proton/Phaze Trilogy (*Split Infinity*, *Blue Adept*, and *Juxtaposition*) consciously blends of the traditions of fantasy and science fiction. In addition, he has written fiction and non-fiction ranging from the Jason Striker series of martial arts thrillers, in collaboration with Roberto Fuentes, to documented essays on diabetes and education for disabled children. His fiction shows a breadth of imagination and invention surpassed by few. And his achievements have been recognized in the form of multiple nominations for Hugo and Nebula awards and other awards, including the August Derleth Award for the best fantasy novel of 1977, *A Spell for Chameleon*.

Yet Anthony's name is as likely to draw disparagement as praise from readers, critics, fans, and fellow writers. Some, like Lin Carter, simply refuse to read anything he has written; [1] others are offended by what they consider his arrogance and obstinacy. He has been involved in contract disputes with publishers and editors; the earliest of these resulted in his being blacklisted by one publisher and his withdrawal from the Science Fiction Writers of America. Anthony is aware that his reputation as a personality has damaged his standing as a writer. In a recent letter, he admits that, as a result of his differences of opinion, "there are reviews I don't get and awards-rosters my books do not get on." [2] Yet he views these difficulties as a measure of his commitment to artistic, professional, and personal standards. Like many of his characters, he refuses to back down when threatened:

I do know how to fight . . . . I don't think I've ever lost a battle in fandom, though my positions have been misrepresented many times . . . . There are a number of people who don't like me—but the root of it has generally been my objection to their standards, rather than the other way around. [3]

In the long run, these controversies have had a beneficial effect on his writing, leading to a toughness and independence of conception and execution that otherwise might not have been possible.

A second consideration essential to understanding Anthony's fiction is the extent to which it reflects his life. He is particularly open about the influence of childhood upon his development as a writer—and, in fact, upon his decision to become a science-fiction writer. He underwent a series of physical and emotional traumas that helped to define both his character and his vocation. In speaking of the role of isolation and disruption in the lives of science-fiction writers, and as a stimulus to the production of science fiction, Brian Aldiss notes of Asimov that "The abrupt uprooting in early childhood sets him in a class with Mary Shelley, Nerval, Wells, Stapledon, Ballard, Aldiss, and many others." [4] The same may be said of Piers Anthony.

Born in Oxford, England, in 1934, Anthony experienced the first major change in his life when his family moved to Spain in 1939. The move represented a tremendous disruption, not so much because of the physical move as because of Anthony's discovery that (as he puts it) "my beloved nurse was not my mother, and that I had to go away with two comparative strangers who were my real parents." [5] In August, 1940, following Alfred Jacob's imprisonment by Franco's government, the family left Spain, an experience even more devastating to the young Anthony than the first had been:

. . . this was my second uprooting, going to a new country with another language, and I suffered. I had a string of psychological problems such as bed-wetting, convulsive head and hand motions and fear of the dark. A single nightmare terrified me for three years. [6]

This experience is reflected in the psychological problems suffered by many of Anthony's heroes, most particularly Brother Paul in the Planet of Tarot trilogy.

The third crisis was emotional: the divorce of his parents when he was eighteen. His childhood had been emotionally bleak, to the point that he has stated that by his eighteenth birthday "had my life ended there, I would have preferred not to have been born." [7]

His attitude was paradoxically compounded and ameliorated by yet another critical event, one which similarly recurs in various forms in his fiction:

When I was 16 my closest cousin, age 15, who had everything to live for, died of cancer; it really seemed unfair, since obviously *I* was the one who should have gone. It was as though I had to justify my life somehow. And so this compulsion to figure it out, to understand why I *did* live, and to make that clear to the world—assuming there was a rationale for it. By the time I had figured the things I needed to know, I was a vegetarian—because of my aversion to death, which I suppose may be taken as a positive sign after my prior attitude—and I was able to express complex thoughts pretty well. So—I wrote. I am an SF writer today because without SF and writing I would be nothing at all today. [8]

The reference to vegetarianism is a prime example of the way Anthony's life informs his novels. *Omnivore* is an extended dissection and justification of vegetarianism, and one of the principal characters, Veg (the name is *not* coincidental), reaches his decision as the result of an experience almost identical to Anthony's. As recently as *Thousandstar* (1980), his characters continue to debate the debilitating effects of a carnivorous or an omnivorous diet.

Anthony took his resolve to write with great seriousness. He wrote a novel as his B.A. thesis for Goddard College (1956); portions of it were later substantially revised and incorporated into *Sos the Rope*. From the beginning, he showed his characteristic energy and intensity. He wrote extensively for fanzines, both before and after becoming a professional (unfortunately, many of his contributions have virtually disappeared). In 1967-1968, he published *Chthon*, *Omnivore*, *Sos the Rope*, *The Ring* (in collaboration with Margroff), and six short stories, which range from direct, uncomplicated narratives to innovative, convoluted treatments of time and space. In 1969, *Macroscope* appeared, which attempts nothing less than an explication of galactic history and takes as its province the entire Milky Way and beyond. The stamina required to write a novel such as *Macroscope* is tremendous, as Anthony is well aware. And again, he seems to model many of his characters after himself; invariably they are physically active and often extraordinarily healthy. In the world of Chthon, for example, there simply *is* no illness. And although Anthony is diabetic, he is nonetheless adamant that a writer must maintain physical strength and stamina:

Irrelevant as it may seem, when I chat about exercise, I actually am answering a question you will get to in due course: how is it that I maintain an output whose quantity (now about 300,000 words of publishable material a year) and (I hope) quality compares favorably with that of the majority of writers. Answer: because ill-health, whether of acute or chronic nature, does not interfere with my writing. [9]

This attitude leads directly, for example, to Flint of Outworld's obsessive concern in *Cluster* that he be transferred into healthy bodies.

In addition to his tendency to incorporate his own experiences into fiction, Anthony has developed several recurring themes and motifs. He consistently defines the dangers modern society poses to its own environment:

> Professionally, I want a halfway decent world for my children to go out into. What I perceive is disquieting. We are not headed for any utopia. It isn't just a matter of corruption and moneygrubbing; there has always been that, and though I don't approve, the world will no doubt survive it. It is that we cannot maintain our present trends without destroying the world as we know it. Food, energy, the environment—we're running out of them all. Our grandchildren may starve and shiver and cough, with no recourse. [10]

These fears result in the almost incessant repetition of the image of Ragnarok—indeed, of the word itself—in most of his fiction. Although the threat of a world-destroying cataclysm has faded from his later work, there is still the underlying problem of energy—the cause, for example, of the crises in the Cluster novels. Throughout his fiction, Anthony presents the problems of individuals, or small groups of individuals, struggling to save their*worlds from depredation by unthinking masses, trying to help the human race learn from the ecological and environmental disasters suffered by other galactic sentients, or establishing parameters by which humans can co-exist with other sentients, as in the recent *Mutes* (1981).

A second trait in his fiction is his flamboyant, often eccentric sense of humor. Even in his most serious work, there is always a trace of humor—situational, verbal, or structural. Names are frequently puns, and plays on words and verbal inversions occur incessantly. He enjoys reversing the reader's expectations—and in fact, inversions of norms (both societal and literary) are common. He challenges the reader to adapt to new situations created by inversions, as when Aton falls in love with the Minionette in *Chthon*. Sadly, for the Minionette, an overt expression of love is a horrible torture, while cruelty is tenderness.

The ability of his characters to adjust to new situations created by the inversions leads to a third consistent element, his concern for maturity, a logical outgrowth of Anthony's own background and his perception of the cultural immaturity that threatens human existence. His imagination ranges from individual struggles toward maturity, such as Aton's in *Chthon* or Ivo Archer's in *Macroscope*; to maturity among races and species, as in the Omnivore series, or *Race Against Time*; to maturity within galaxies and galactic clusters, as in the quest for soul-sapience in the Cluster series. His focus varies widely— literally from the microcosm to the macrocosm.

In addition to these broad tendencies in his fiction, there are several lesser concerns that deserve mention. He consistently uses mythology, literary allusions, and legends to give life and variety to his episodes; he explores such non-science-fiction elements as the Tarot, astrology, and theology; he explores with unusual tenacity the concept of aura, not only the Kirlian auras of the Cluster series, but a more amorphous sense implicit in nearly every novel and short story. His characters, while rarely stereotyped, tend to share similar traits: they are young, either emotionally or physically; they are often small, reflecting Anthony's own stature, or physically inhibited (there are of course exceptions to this generalization, especially in *Battle Circle*). Their enemies tend to be their own ignorance (again and again, Anthony refers to knowledge as a tradable commodity); more frequently than not, the enemy the immature hero initially defines turns out to be, if not an outright ally, at least neutral (*The Ring*, *Blue Adept*, *Juxtaposition*) and manipulated by a third party. His societies frequently condone nakedness—not for any easy titillation of the reader (his characters know that total, habitual nakedness reduces rather than heightens sexual interest), but rather as a way of literally stripping them of their pretensions and preoccupations and allowing them to develop anew. Closely related to the restrained sexuality implicit in nudity is his frequent use of sterility, barrenness, and castration to highlight a character's illusions about life. Children occur rarely in his novels; when they do appear, they signal an unusual victory of the protagonists over the forces of chaos, immaturity, and destruction.

Of course, an introductory study such as this can not hope to capture more than the highlights in a writer as varied and prolific as Anthony. Nor can it profess to do more than suggest elements that the reader might find valuable. In addition, before it sees print, it will probably be outdated, since Anthony continues to publish at an enormous rate. However, as he has noted, "That's the problem in dealing with a writer whose career is not safely over." [11] And to compound the difficulty, his recent interests have begun to swing away from science fiction. One project includes World War II fiction.

Regardless of the limitations of this study, however, there is much that needs to be said about Anthony's writing to date. He is highly imaginative, but at the same time self-consistent; much of what is said about one novel is applicable to others. He is a careful craftsman in his plotting and in creating an array of truly alien characters. The entry under his name in *A Reader's Guide to Science Fiction* provides a balanced assessment of his strengths:

> Piers Anthony is one of those authors who can perform magic with the ordinary; he manages to take what at first glance seems to be a fairly pedestrian plot and make of it something rather special . . . . Anthony is a craftsman, and, like a skilled furniture builder who can make a chair much more than a

place to sit, makes a book more than words to read. Don't be misled by plot summary of any of his works; even if it sounds like you may have read it before by another author. Anthony will give you something extra. [12]

That something is frequently an irrepressible sense of fun, of excitement, and of energy.

Not everyone responds as favorably to Anthony's "furniture," of course. A recent review of *Split Infinity* concentrates (too much, it seems) on his weaknesses:

> Unfortunately, Anthony has little sense of style or rhythm. This is how he describes Stile riding a unicorn he hopes to tame: "The unicorn's feet touched the snow. Steam puffed up from that contact. She really had hot feet!" That gratuitous last statement, exclamation point included, is one of many such sentences.
>
> The plot is incomplete and cross-eyed—staring in two directions, hobbled by expository lumps. [13]

Admittedly, Anthony's style is frequently uneven, but just as frequently, the stylistic lapses are overcome by the freshness and energy of his imagination. Ian Watson captured this sense of ambivalence when he wrote:

> I'm interested in Piers Anthony. Now he's another appalling writer who deals with very interesting themes. He turns out a trilogy a week, as far as I can see, and continually I read them, conscious of the appalling flaws, but really rather interested. [14]

As a final assessment of Anthony, it seems justifiable to suggest that Anthony is a writer whose works have suffered unjustly because of his reputation—a reputation having little to do with the merits of his fiction. He has been slighted critically, receiving little attention for books that are novel and exciting. As an individual, Anthony belies much that is unofficially rumored about him: he has been generous in his cooperation in the preparation of this study, his attitude never once suggesting the arrogance or bellicosity he is supposed to exhibit. But even Anthony would, I think, argue that such personal considerations are out of place. He is dedicated to his writing and demands that he be judged by its merits, and on that alone. And on that basis, he should rank among the most individual, original, and thought-provoking science-fiction writers today.

NOTES

1.   Lin Carter has said simply, "I don't read Piers Anthony. Wouldn't read Piers Anthony if you paid me." ("Lin Carter Interview continued," *Science Fiction Times* [May 1980], p. 9.

2.   Letter to Michael R. Collings, 13 May 1980.

3.   Cliff Biggers, "An Interview with Piers Anthony," *Science Fiction Review*, November 1977, p. 60.

4.   *This World and Nearer Ones: Essays Exploring the Familiar* (Kent, Ohio: Kent State University Press, 1981), p.33.

5.   Biggers, p. 56. Additional biographical data is available in the headnote to "In the Barn" in *Again, Dangerous Visions*, ed. Harlan Ellison (Garden City, New York: Doubleday, 1972), pp. 385-392.

6.   Biggers, p. 56.

7.   Biggers, p. 57.

8.   Biggers, p. 57. In the letter of May 13, 1980, Anthony indicated that a knowledge of his background "relates more intimately to my published work than anyone who does not know me is likely to suspect."

9.   Letter to Michael R. Collings, 7 June 1980.

10.   Biggers, p. 61.

11.   Letter, 13 May 1980.

12.   Baird Searles, *et al. A Reader's Guide to Science Fiction* (New York: Avon, 1979), pp. 9-10.

13.   Mel Gilden, "Sturgeon's Law Upheld by a Cross-Eyed Tale," *Los Angeles Times Book Review*, 17 August 1980, p. 7. Gilden seems unaware that *Split Infinity* is a trilogy; he concludes his review by saying,

> At the happy ending, we still don't even know who Stile's enemies are. The evidence suggests Anthony forced two novellas to mate at gunpoint.

By misreading the intent of the novel, Gilden entirely overlooks the stated purpose—to blend science fiction and fantasy through the device of having Stile, the hero, cross from one world to its fantasy alternate. Many of the negative reponses to Anthony's works reveal similar shortsightedness as to the author's purposes.

14.   *Dream Makers*, ed. Charles Platt (New York: Berkley, 1980), p. 239.

III

BATTLE CIRCLE

Battle Circle is an ideal place to begin a discussion of Anthony's novels. The trilogy begins with an early novel, *Sos the Rope*, which, although not his first published novel, is a re-working of his 1956 B.A. thesis, "The Unstilled World." [1] The two remaining novels—*Var the Stick* (1972) and *Neq the Sword* (1975)—complement the earlier work and, in conjunction with *Sos*, offer insights into nearly two decades of Anthony's development.

A reader first coming to *Battle Circle* is tempted to consider the trilogy simply as another stereotyped science-fiction novel detailing the decline of human society into barbarism after the inevitable atomic or nuclear holocaust. Superficially, at least, there seems some justification for such a judgment. The cover blurb on the Avon edition fairly shouts at the reader in terms appropriate to the ninety percent of science fiction that Sturgeon's Law dictates is of poor quality:

> America rising from the ashes of its final destruction—the epic story of the savage struggle for empire and dominance in primitive post-cataclysmic America.

Reviewers have been seduced by this superficial sense of the stereotypic into treating *Battle Circle*—and its individual novels—as too easily predictable, as simplistic and slavishly adhering to the reader's expectations. According to one review of *Var*,

> . . . it is the same postholocaust setting [as *Sos*], with America reduced to wandering nomad barbarians (whose men are known by their weapons) and a small underground of technologically knowledgeable types. The techies maintain the nomads as a safety valve for the belligerent strain of humanity, to prevent another blow-up. [2]

The review ignores, or at the least passes over as trivial, much that is complex and sophisticated. The wording—i.e., "wandering nomad

16

barbarians," "technologically knowledgeable types," and "techies"—suggests a slickness to *Var*, and by extension to the trilogy, a conclusion that is both hasty and unjust. Referring to the complexly interdependent social structure of *Battle Circle* in terms of nomad barbarians and techies not only obscures the tripartite division of that society (with each division essentially dependent upon, while often unknowingly contributing to, the others), but also ignores one of Anthony's most pervasive themes: the necessity for division and external control of individuals and societies not sufficiently mature to monitor their own decisions and activities. Without such controls, *Battle Circle* argues, humanity is unremittingly self-destructive. Remove those controls entirely, and social conventions crumble. [3]

This theme develops explicitly in the opening chapters of *Sos*, the first volume of the trilogy. Sos guides Sol of All Weapons and Sol's woman Soli into the fringes of radioactive badlands to begin forming the core of an empire to replace the loose tribal structure of the nomads. They establish a base camp in a seemingly perfect location, a shallow valley near a lake, ideal as a training ground and apparently uncontaminated by lingering radiation, although inexplicably barren of any surface life. They discover the cause of the barrenness, however, when their camp is overrun by millions of shrews. The vicious animals attack like a "grey carpet . . . spreading over the hill and sliding grandly toward the plain, as though some cosmic jug were spilling thick oil upon the landscape" (Ch. 3). Sos identifies them for Soli; they are mammals, he says, and mammals are "the most savage and versatile vertebrates on Earth." The horde is unstoppable; it literally scours the surface of the area, consuming all other life-forms and forcing the humans to flee for their lives. Ultimately, the shrews depart to seek new sources of food. If they remain in one area too long, they will starve themselves. The horde literally destroys itself by its rapaciousness and by the sheer mass of bodies. [4]

The invasion of the shrews provides Anthony with an opportunity to move the plot forward several steps, primarily by throwing Sos and Soli together. But even more importantly, the shrews serve as an initial emblem for another mammal, one potentially more dangerous yet, especially when massed in uncontrollable numbers—man. In the final chapter of *Sos*, Sos returns from a self-imposed exile in Mount Helicon. He returns nameless and weaponless (name and weapon are inextricably linked in the world of *Battle Circle*), surgically altered into the greatest warrior of all, to confront Sol and contend for mastery of the Empire. Sos does not desire personal prestige, however; his express purpose is to destroy the empire which, like the horde of shrews, is ultimately destructive. When he speaks to the assembled warriors, he carefully defines the potentials of too centralized a civilization:

> Now you travel in large tribes and you fight for other men
> when they tell you to. You till the land, working as the crazies

do, because your numbers are too great for the resources of any one area. You mine for metals, because you no longer trust the crazies to do it for you, though they have never broken trust. You study from books, because you want the things civilization can offer. But this is not the way it should be. We know what civilization leads to. It brings destruction of all the values of the circle. It brings competition for material things you do not need. Before long you will overpopulate the Earth and become a scourge upon it, like shrews who have overrun their feeding grounds.

The records show that the end result of empire is—the Blast. (Ch. 20) [5]

Given the context of *Battle Circle*, Sos is correct. Sol's empire continues, even after the champion's defeat in the circle, but only because Sos is convinced that Helicon is an even greater danger than the Empire. Finally, Sos unleashes the power of the Empire to destroy Helicon, a man-made slag mountain harboring those who guard hollow remnants of pre-Blast technology and who preserve such irrelevancies as televisions with pictures but no sound and interminable commercials for products long since faded even from the memories of men. Sos fears the potential destructiveness of *any* source of centralized power, while simultaneously realizing that man's most potent enemy is himself. Once before, human society had

grown phenomenally numerous and strong, and had resided in cities where every conceivable (and inconceivable) comfort of life was available. Then these fabulously prosperous peoples had destroyed it all in a rain of fire, a smash of intolerable radiation, leaving only the scattered nomads and crazies and underworlders, and the extensive badlands. (*Var*, Ch. 2)

Such insanity is nearly incomprehensible, even to Sos, now the "Nameless One," who has dwelt for a time among all three divisions of society—nomads, crazies, and underworlders—and consequently understands more of human history than any of the others. The great paradox developed throughout *Battle Circle* is quite simply that as man becomes more civilized, he destroys that which makes him civilized. [6]

After the destruction of Helicon, men again descend into uncontrolled barbarism, and the Empire dies by attrition. The battle circle code, the sole form of control, disappears, leaving only soul-destroying ugliness and brutality in its place. Neq's experiences in the final volume point explicitly to the underlying nature of man, once he is stripped of any internal or external controls. Neq himself becomes a silent killer, murdering tens of innocents out of an impulse for revenge.

Near the end of the trilogy, however, Helicon is re-inhabited, cleaned and purified both physically and morally, and the complex relationship between Helicon, the crazies, and the nomads is restored. Anthony restates his theme, defining the need for man to divorce himself from his shrew-like past by (temporarily, at least) limiting the dissemination of technical knowledge and simultaneously providing an outlet for man's inherently violent nature:

> The nomads were the real future of mankind. The crazies were only the caretakers, preserving what they could of the civilization the nomads would one day draw upon. Helicon was the supplier of the crazies. But Helicon and the crazies could not make the civilization themselves, for that would be identical to the system of the past.
>
> The past that had made the Blast. The most colossal failure in man's history.
>
> Yet by the same token the nomads had to be prevented from assuming command of Helicon, either to destroy it or to absorb its technology directly. There must not be a forced choice between barbarism and the Blast. The caretaker order had to be maintained for centuries, perhaps millenia, until the nomads, in their own time, outgrew it. Then the new order would truly prevail, shed of the liabilities of the old. (*Neq*, Ch. 18)

The battle circle becomes another manifestation of the ring worn by lawbreakers in *The Ring*, or the complex structure of alien overlordship in *Triple Detente*, except that here, *all* men are ultimately law-breakers, either actually (as in Neq's case) or potentially. The battle-circle/ring/ overlord forcefully circumscribes men until they have matured to the point that they can circumscribe themselves. Neq's awareness of this principle is in itself the first step toward such a maturity.

Anthony's indictment of civilization is the obverse of his indictment of the "natural" man. Man in isolation is brutal and violent, animalistically aggressive; man in the aggregate is self-destructive as a species. Without the order imposed by the battle circle, man becomes simply destructive, a destructivity paralleled by a sexuality divorced from potential reproduction.

Sexuality is an important motif in Anthony's fictions, usually as a normal, healthy quality in human beings. Within the battle-circle society, sex and sexual roles are clearly defined by passing and possessing a warrior's bracelet. The woman assumes a derivative of her warrior's name as she accepts his bracelet (a figurative ring as binding and controlled as the battle circle itself). Her child will bear that man's name—regardless of who the biological father might actually be—but within the battle circle society the exchange of bracelets represents a virtually inviolable covenant. Var and Neq both face nearly insuperable difficulties as a result of their inability to pass their bracelets; and Sos's antipathy toward the Empire and Helicon stems in part from his estrangement from his child, who bears the name Soli, and in part from his paradoxical dedication to the circle code he and Sola had broken. The passing of the bracelet is not permanent, however, and a woman may bear several names during her lifetime. The complexities of sexual and parental roles are essential to the plot of *Battle Circle*, since they mirror in small the complexities of the larger society. Potentially destructive emotions and interrelationships are kept in check—controlled—by the tenuous yet rigid restrictions of the bracelets. When the circle code disappears in *Neq*, all respect for the bracelet simultaneously disappears. A prisoner of men no longer bound by the circle code, Neq must watch his wife raped. And the leader of the tribe consciously breaks with the bracelet tradition:

> Han glanced at Neqa, then guiltily away again. "But she's—she has his bracelet!"
> "Yeah. That's funny. Leave it on."
> "But—"
> "He's going to watch this. On his own band. That's his punishment. And some of hers." (Ch. 7).

Sexuality and reproduction are thus images of larger patterns in the trilogy. Controlled, they are essential to man's continuation; uncontrolled, left to the impulses of man, they become merely additional instruments of destruction and death.

Significantly, nearly every main character in the three volumes fails to propagate legal children, and in almost every instance because of the instrusion of technology into human life. As a child, Sol had been castrated and mutilated in intertribal conflicts stemming from the disruption of society following the Blast. The crazies saved his life but could not restore his potency. From the beginning, as Sos realizes clearly, Sol's dreams of empire are literally fruitless; he will have no heir to follow him and sustain his conquests. Sos, in turn, fathers a child by Sola; the child, Soli, however, legally belongs to Sol and, when Sos defeats Sol, she follows her "father" to exile on Helicon. Sos remains in fact childless; thus, the nascent Empire dies under the control of the Nameless One, who remains interested in it only as long as it offers some hope that he might eventually regain possession of his biological daughter. Ultimately, both Sos and Sol sacrifice themselves so their daughter might survive. Sola escapes with Var into the wilderness and begins a long trek homeward.

Yet Var does not insure the propagation of the race, even after the self-sacrifice of the two greatest warriors of the age. He is a child of the badlands; his mottled, radiation-sensitive skin and misshapen limbs mark him as a mutant. But even deeper is the most devastating legacy of a civilization beyond control—because of his exposure to radiation, he is sterile. Even after he places his bracelet on Soli—now to be known as Vara—there is no hope for a new generation. As Vara laments,

". . . I have nothing. Not even vengeance . . . . Not even his child." For Var was sterile. Her father Sol had been castrate; she had been conceived on his bracelet by Sos the Rope, who later gave his own bracelet to Sosa at Helicon. So her husband, like her father had had no child. (*Neq*, Ch. 15)

The motif of castration/sterility/impotence continues through most of the final volume, *Neq the Sword* (and recurs frequently in Anthony's other works). Neq, who is physically capable of generation, is psychologically unable to approach a woman until he finally places his bracelet on Miss Smith. But before their relationship can be consummated, she is raped and killed, and Neq is punished for trying to save her: both his hands are severed at the wrist. After literally grafting a sword onto the stump of his arm—thus becoming in fact Neq the Sword—he begins his campaign of vengeance and retribution. He is single-mindedly destructive, killing viciously and coldly, with no regard for innocence or guilt. In the course of his wanderings, he encounters and kills Var; then, in expiation, he must father a child on Vara. And again, the resulting child is not his, but legally Var's.

In each stage of the chronicle of the decline and fall of the circle society, then, Anthony's heroes are either sterile, barren, or allowed to father only biologically, never legally. And, by analogy, the societies that each interacts with are sterile, self-destructive, ultimately both suicidal and genocidal. Within the Empire, as Sos and Sol discover, children complicate rather than resolve problems. And outside of it, as Var and Neq discover, reproductive sexuality is displaced by ungoverned lust and resultant death. Only at the end of the trilogy, as Neq oversees the reconstruction of Helicon and the restoration of the tripartite nomad-crazies-underworlder society, does Anthony allow the promise of fertility. Children, as images of man's ability to overcome his destructive urges, emerge only as Neq restores both stability and control by re-creating the intricate "checks and balances" that make human society possible. Through Neq, order and harmony, as epitomized by the perfect form of the battle circle itself, are restored.

Given this emphasis on order and control, on the disastrous results of collisions between disparate world views, it is not surprising to discover that Anthony structures the three novels on patterns provided by perhaps the most traditional, order-conscious, and controlled of literary forms, the epic. One outstanding feature of the trilogy is its overriding shape. Each of the three component novels carries Anthony's account of the gradual disintegration and reintegration of a complex yet tenuous social order a few stages further. Taken as a whole, the novels reinforce the sense that the reader is observing the actions of men and women who, to borrow Frye's distinction, differ from common men in degree, but not in kind. [7] They are larger-than-life and as muscular as the Adam of the Sistine chapel and just as far removed from the reader's everyday experience. Yet they remain men and women, not gods or demi-urges. They are, in a word, epical.

This sense is reinforced by the presence in *Battle Circle* of a number of conventions traditionally associated most strongly with the epic. Initially, the most obvious of these is the sense throughout of cultures in conflict, of violent confrontation between the new and the old. And the confrontation and the warfare between the forces of change and those of tradition and order imply (as is common in the epic) world-wide consequences. The cultures in question are branches from a trunk already proven rotten by history; it is part of Anthony's strategy to force the present (the nomads) to confront the past (Helicon and the underworld), and from that confrontation to create a new, more stable social order which, like Aeneas's Rome, will survive for centuries.

In addition to the epic milieu of the trilogy, Anthony's definition of the hero also shares much with that of the epic hero. His heroes are superior to common men (as noted above), not in kind, but in degree. Sol, Sos, and Neq are superlatives among warriors; Sol, in fact, is Sol of All Weapons, the single champion, proficient at all weapons allowed in the battle circle. Var is competent with his sticks, but even more importantly, he is uniquely suited to survival in a world still poisoned by residual radiation. As one reads *Sos*, *Var*, or *Neq*, the heroes seem to grow larger, until they are far beyond their fellows—the stuff of myths and legends. As Tyl the Sword says late in the trilogy, speaking to Sola and Soli/Vara:

> You both knew Var well. And Sol. And the Weaponless.
> As I did. Soon we must talk together of great men. (*Neq*,
> Ch. 17)

Among these heroes, as among most epic characters, name and reputation are critical. The fall and rebirth of the circle code is initiated in hand-to-hand combat, significantly and appropriately over the right to the name *Sol*, claimed by rival warriors. [8] Throughout *Sos*, there is a constant emphasis on name, to the extent that in a rather Miltonic inversion, men are named after the weapons they wield, [9] thus, "Sos the Rope," "Neq the Sword," and others. In a twist again Miltonic and ironic, Sol of All Weapons is defeated by the greatest warrior of all, Sos, now surgically altered by the technicians of Helicon to enhance his physical abilities and hide his identity. [10] He returns as the anti-hero, the Nameless and the Weaponless. In his new manifestation, Sos works against the Empire, against Helicon, and against a world that invites epic grandeur and pretentions—and by doing so becomes himself an epic hero.

It is also conventional in epics that the action be divided into separate parts; Milton, for example, may have broken the original ten books of *Paradise Lost* into twelve at least in part because by doing so, he would bring his work closer to the duodecimal structure of the *Aeneid*. And within Milton's twelve-book structure, *Paradise Lost* divides neatly into a trilogy: Books I-IV, dealing primarily with Satan, God, and Eden; Books V-VIII, a recital of past events; and Books IX-XII, dealing with the Fall and Restoration to Grace. *Battle Circle* is, of course, overtly a trilogy, one which investigates the viability of three fundamental forms of epic: the Achilean epic of martial prowess; the Odyssean epic of wandering; and the Virgillian/Miltonic epic of self-sacrifice and restoration.

Sos resembles the *Iliad* in being replete with formal, hand-to-hand combat; in showing an unusual emphasis on name, reputation, and weaponry; in defining the giving and receiving of rings (bracelets) as visible symbols of manhood and military proficiency; and in describing a warfare-morality that decrees honorable death within the circle to be infinitely preferrable to a long, inactive life outside it. The novel even includes a reflection of the archetypal descent into the underworld for enlightenment, although as is so typical in Anthony's prose, the image is inverted. To reach the underworld, Sos must ascend Mt. Helicon, an imagistic conflation of Homer's underworld and Milton's mountain of revelation. The primary actions in *Sos* center around the carving out of an empire form the ruins of a fallen society, and the final discovery that the empire created to ensure order is itself the instrument of disorder and chaos. The Illiadic warfare proves, in the end, as hollow and meaningless as the burned-out shell of Helicon.

Var the Stick abandons the Achillean/Illiadic format for an overtly Odyssean structure. Again inverting the reader's expectations, Anthony first presents Var as little better than a beast, who gradually gains in humanity and dignity only when he abandons the hopelessness and emptiness of the empire and its fruitless siege of Helicon and strikes out with his former opponent, the girl Soli, to wander throughout the wilderness of Northern America, across the Bering Sea, finally to China. Like Odysseus, Var and Soli encounter wonders and marvels: an Amazonian hive-culture; a genetic mutation designed to recapitulate the Cretan Minotaur in both form and lust; an exotic and decadent oriental court; and everywhere, inescapable traces of the Blast.

During their wanderings, they discover not only their full maturity as individuals and—in Var's case, at least—their humanity, but they also underscore Anthony's thesis that humanity needs external controls over his behavior. The series of adventures suggests alternatives for controlling man's agressiveness. Lacking the triple "checks and balances" system of circle society, other societies become skewed, oppressive, inhuman as one element—i.e., the bee-like women, the megalosexual minotaur and his captor-priests, the ineffectual Chinese aristocracy—assumes leadership and, like the morally twisted Bob in Helicon, distorts society to conform to one individual's desires. In this sense, Var's wandering as not as irrelevant as at least one critic has suggested; they are not a breaking away from the main thread of the trilogy, but rather part of Anthony's investigation of alternatives, leading to a final development in circle society. As Soli/Vara states:

There are other Helicons in other parts of the world, but they were never as good as ours and they don't have much effect. Var and I discovered that in the years we traveled. To the north they have guns and electricity, but they are not nice people. In Asia they have trucks and ships and buildings, but they—well, for us, our way is best. So now we are going to rebuild Helicon . . . . (*Neq*, Ch. 18)

Var does not return home, however, to the healthy and prosperous old age of an Odysseus. *Var* breaks off at a literal turning point in the wanderings, as Soli's fathers (legal and biological), maimed and sold into slavery, sacrifice themselves to save Var and Soli. In *Neq*, the opening chapters relate the experiences of Neq and his companion, Miss Smith, in a world suddenly deprived of a coherent code of behavior. After Miss Smith's/Neqa's brutal death, Neq devotes himself to vengeance, like the monomaniacal hero of a martial epic, only to discover that vengeance is insufficient. He encounters Var (who suddenly seems to the reader beast-like and slow). Still believing that Var had killed Soli during the siege of Helicon, Neq challenges and kills Var. Maddened by his own loss, Neq destroys the happiness of the innocent. Then, after a long and painful period of self-examination and remorse, he vows to rebuild what has been destroyed. Like his literary progenitors, Aeneas and Adam, Neq first loses all—including in this instance his honor—and then dedicates himself to the reconstruction of order from chaos. He replaces the prosthetic swords with a glockenspiel and hammer and emerges from the anarchy of Sol's fallen empire to rebuild Helicon on a firm, sane, stable base.

Battle Circle, then, is more complex than it might at first suggest. It is complex in characterization and invention, unusually so for a science-fiction novel. [12] It approaches a difficult theme, and in doing so, engages in a struggle to define human nature itself. As Paul McGuire concludes:

In repose as sharp as a nomad's sword, and as stark as their lives, Anthony writes of the prices of heroism, the power of love, the futility of vengeance, and the weight of responsibility. It is often brutal, but beautiful in the realization of its ambitious scope. [13]

NOTES:

1. *Sos* was the winner of the 1968, $5000 Science Fiction Novel Award, sponsored by Pyramid, *The Magazine of Fantasy and Science Fiction*, and Kent Productions. The original version, "The Unstilled World," is available (with Anthony's written permission) in microfilm from Goddard College.
2. *Publishers Weekly*, 15 October 1973, pp. 63-64.

3.   Anthony returns to this theme frequently, most notably in *Triple Detente*, which provides a harsh but intriguing solution to the problems of overpopulation, depletion of resources, and human insensitivity to environment; in *But What of Earth?*, which posits a sudden depletion in Earth's population because of the development of a mattermitter; in *The Ring*, which like Burgess's *Clockwork Orange* investigates artificial methods of monitoring human impulses, but unlike Burgess's novel concludes that such external aids, properly devised, are essential for the smooth functioning of human society; and to a lesser extent in the Jason Striker martial arts novels, in which the martial arts themselves become a means for controlling aggressiveness.

4.   Here, as in *But What of Earth?*, *Triple Detente*, and *The Ring*, Anthony is indebted to Calhoun's experiments relating to the behavior of rats subjected to artificially created overcrowding. Frank Herbert's *The Dosadi Experiment* (1977) seems similarly based on Calhoun's experiments and arrives at similar conclusions to Anthony's novels; the stress involved is deadly, but the survivors are strengthened by their trials.

Calhoun's findings, beginning with the publication of "The Study of Wild Animals under Controlled Conditions," (*Annals of the New York Academy of Sciences*, 51 [1950], pp. 113-122) are discussed at length in Edward T. Hall's *The Hidden Dimension* (New York: Doubleday, 1966), Chapter III, "Crowding and Social Behavior in Animals."

5.   Later, Sos states explicitly, "We are shrews . . . . We must utilize shrew tactics" (*Var*, Ch. 8). Anthony is simultaneously aware, however, of the dangers inherent in a loose tribal society. *Battle Circle*, like *But What of Earth?* and *Rings of Ice*, is no simplistic pastoral constructed on the thesis that if technological civilization is removed, human life will function easily and smoothly. Indeed, Anthony is, at this stage, consciously brutal in his definition of human society without the restraints imposed by civilization; but he ultimately sees the smaller social groups as preferable.

6.   Compare this with Walter Miller's *A Canticle for Leibowitz* (New York: Lippincott, 1959).

7.   Northrop Frye, *Anatomy of Criticism* (1957; rpt. New York: Atheneum, 1967), pp. 33-34.

8.   It is typical of Anthony's humor that *Sol* is a multiple pun; the two warriors fight for sole mastery of the name and, ultimately, of the empire.

9.   Traditionally, the weapons are named by the warriors; Anthony reverses the structure, naming his warriors after the weapons they bear. For an excellent discussion of Milton's inversion of epic conventions, see John M. Steadman, *Milton and the Renaissance Hero* (London: Oxford University Press, 1967).

10. He here touches on yet another convention: the hero in disguise.

11. Paul McGuire, Review of *Battle Circle*, *Science Fiction Review*, 7, No. 2 (May 1978), p. 55.

12. "Anthony concocts an unusual blend of high adventure and rich characterization in *The Battle Circle* trilogy. Set in a post-catastrophic world where a benevolent scientific elite keeps the rest of the populace in ignorant barbarism and nomadic wandering, the three novels, *Sos*, *Var*, and *Neq*, detail intriguing cultures, beliefs and characters, often in violent and well described conflicts." (Searles, *Reader's Guide*, p. 9). Except for the over-simplification of "a scientific elite," Searles' comments seem typical of reactions to the trilogy. Neil Barron (*Anatomy of Wonder: Science Fiction* [New York: R. R. Bowker Company, 1976]) refers to *BC* as "An extremely rare blend of adventure story and rich characterization, incisively plausible incident, reinforcing symbolism, and poignantly evoked theme" (pp. 133-134).
13. McGuire, p. 55.

IV

THE ATON NOVELS:

Chthon and *Phthor*

Chthon was Anthony's first novel sale, although his second to see publication. It is doubly important in his canon, since it not only introduces themes and concerns pertinent to nearly every subsequent novel, but also received critical and popular acclaim unsurpassed by any of his other novels, with the possible exception of *Macroscope*. It received the Nebula nomination in 1967, and the Hugo nomination in 1968, as well as substantial critical attention. The responses immediately pinpointed *Chthon*'s tremendous complexity in plotting, structure and development. Anthony was aware that the book was going to be difficult; he notes in an interview that it took him "seven years to struggle through *Chthon*." [1] But his experiment in time-distortion paid off. According to a review in *Publishers Weekly*, *Chthon* is

> A busy and ingenious combination of the elements of myth, poetry, folk song, symbolism, suspense story—a bursting package, almost too much for one book, but literate, original, and entertaining. [2]

Leo Harris reiterates this assessment:

> Piers Anthony has created a whole new world, a dream universe which you find yourself living in and, after a while, understanding. Very poetic and tough and allegorical it all is, and it will rapidly have thee in thrall. [3]

Much of what has been said about *Chthon* applies as well to *Phthor*, which expands upon the mythic, poetic, and symbolic intricacy of the first volume.

Chthon is the story of Aton Five, a native of Planet Hvee (and the pun on five/V is intentional). He has been exiled to the prison planet *Chthon*, where he struggles against internal guilt and external dangers,

27

finally forcing his fellow prisoners to make the virtually impossible "Hard Trek" through the lowest caverns of Chthon (read *Hell*). He alone survives to reach the surface. Interwoven with this narrative are chapters recounting his youth and early adulthood: his meeting at seven years of age with the minionette Malice; his subsequent meetings with her; his adventures on the proscribed planet Minion; his return from Chthon to Hvee; his climactic battle with Bedside, the representative of the cavern-deity Chthon; and his surrender/compromise with Chthon and return to the caverns.

Phthor continues the tale a generation later. Arlo, son of Aton, has spent his life in the caverns beneath the old prison. He is protected by a telepathic link with Chthon, the mineral intelligence controlling all sentience in the caverns. Into Arlo's garden-paradise comes Ex, an apparently human girl who initiates Arlo's break with Chthon and the struggle for control of the caverns that evolves into Ragnarok, the cataclysmic battle between the forces of Life and Death. Throughout, Aton appears, as do other characters from *Chthon*, but the story is essentially Arlo's.

Anthony uses a number of themes and devices to augment his narratives. The most immediately obvious is his interweaving of episodes, without respect for chronology, or, in the case of *Phthor*, for reality. The chapters in both novels are arranged by years, but part of the difficulty in reading either of them is that the chapters break with traditional time. *Chthon* begins with Aton's entry into Chthon; jumps back nineteen years to the Hvee farms of family Five; moves ahead to his first experiences in prison; jumps back to his tenure on the space ship *Jocasta* (a name carefully chosen for its mythic and psychological suggestions); then moves again forward to the continuing adventures in the prison. This pattern repeats throughout the novel, and although the actions defined in *Chthon* extend three years after his imprisonment, the novel concludes with Aton's escape from the caverns. Throughout, Anthony distorts the reader's time-sense, referring to events that have not yet occurred in the literal movement of the novel, but which predate the actions being described in the particular passage.

This pattern is repeated in *Phthor* but with even greater care and to greater effect. Anthony develops the image of life as a *Y*, a series of choices leading irrevocably to one of two paths. The Prologue defines the importance of the Y-configuration:

> History of his manifestation as Phthor
> Bifurcate, a figure Y
> Past—Present—Future
> Represented as segments of the limbs
> Four escapes, and none
>
> The only answer
> Destruction

The chapters enlarge the Y-construction, repeating in a chiastic arrangement and leading from front and back to the interlog, the essential statement of Anthony's theme:

Prologue

I.	Chthon		[year] 426
II.	Death		460
III.	War		426
		IV. Tree	
Interlog			[Infinity] ∞
		IV. Tree	
V.	Thor		426
VI.	Life		460
VII.	Phthor		426

Epilog

The interlog diagrams the possibilities open to Arlo, and through him, to the forces of Life and Death:

Yggdrasil   Sentience
Great World Tree   Galactic Habitats
Whose roots extend   Heaven/Purgatory/Hell
Into three realms   Idyllia/Prison/Caverns
The Gods   Aesir-Vanir
The Giants   Zombies
The Dead   Chthon
History of Aton Five's mergence with Chthon
Shape of a Hexagon
Garnet-faceted
Crafted by mineral intellect
History of Arlo's divergence from Chthon
Shape of a Y
Antennae marking bifurcate futures:
Victory of Chthon   Victory of Life
Center marking the decision.
00

As this overview suggests, Anthony consciously manipulates the readers' time-sense to thrust them more completely into the universe of Chthon. The seemingly eccentric fragmentation of time, and its reassembly into a structure resembling a cubist painting, forces the readers' closer involvement with the novel, merely to understand what is happening on the literal level as well as on a number of thematic and symbolic levels.

The most obvious of these levels is the mythic patterning pervading both novels. From the title *Chthon*, through the last word of *Phthor*— "Phthor," a homonym for *Thor*—Anthony weaves a complex tapestry of myth and legend drawn from classical antiquity; from Norseland; from the Christian Eden and Paradise Lost; from Dante's Purgatory; from the modern mythologies of psychoanalysis and psychology; from literature; and from folk tales of magicians and dragons. All of the strands are to closely patterned that eventually the characters themselves lose sight of the differences between reality and legend and begin living myths as if they were the reality, while thinking about their own realities as mythic.

Chthon relies heavily on classical mythology. The minionettes are modeled, for example, on the Sirens. They are unique, embodiments of ultimate womanhood, telepathic (but with inverted reception, perceiving love as hate, hate as love), virtually identical progeny of a single cloned stock, and exclusively incestuous. The minionette bears a son who will eventually kill his father and in turn father a son upon his own mother; that son will kill *his* father. Since the minionettes may live for hundreds of years, the line of incest continues unbroken until the minionette intuits her own death and bears a daughter. After her death, her daughter will mate with the father/brother and bear him a son, continuing the line.

Aton Five is half-minion. The elusive woman he seeks is, he discovers, his own mother, Malice (note the inversion implicit in the name). She appears to him twice in the fields of Hvee, but the critical encounter occurs aboard the *Jocasta*. Eventually, Aton rapes Malice, unknowingly fathering the minionette Vex (introduced in *Phthor* as Ex), who is irresistibly attracted to both Arlo, her half-brother, and Aton, her father/brother.

The myth of Oedipus shapes Aton's internal struggles. He is no more capable of resisting the imperatives of his heredity than Oedipus was of circumventing the oracles. Aton is aware of his figurative blindness in his relationship with Malice and eventually recognizes the name of the ship as a signal, "intended to guide him to her when he was mature enough to understand" (Ch. V). Later, in *Phthor*, Oedipus is complemented by Electra as Vex is caught between her desire for and promises to Arlo, and her uncontrollable genetic attraction for her father, Aton. In Arlo's vision of the victory of Life over Death, he has killed his father Aton to possess Vex, and nearly thirty years later, he attempts to kill his son to keep the youth from possessing Vex.

In addition, *Chthon* makes clear and careful references to Tantalus, the Sphinx, and the Chimera. The prison-complex suggests the classical world view itself. During the "Hard Trek," Aton realizes that Chthon is a closed system, composed of the "fire cycle," the "world of water," the self-regenerating cycles of gas and air, and the surrounding earth.

Only just less prominent than classical references are references to

Dante. The prison of Chthon is immediately suggestive of Dante's Hell, with its circles (the caverns and passageways are described frequently as being exactly circular) and its intensifying tortures the deeper into its circles one passes. Yet like so many other things in Anthony's imagination, Hell (as defined by Chthon) is an inversion of Heaven. Aton discovers that the prison is located beneath Idyllia, the Edenic garden-planet that serves as a healing-place and a place of restoration and regeneration.

In the lowest cavern of Chthon, inhabited by prisoners incapable of living at peace even with other prisoners (and no one is sent to Chthon except the most incorrigible of criminals), Aton paradoxically discovers no evil—save in himself. He finds only men and women intent on surviving, living according to a strict code of ethics, and respecting each other's privacy and integrity. They wear no clothing, because of the oppressive heat of the cavern winds; yet there is no rape until Aton arrives. The prisoners are rudimentarily armed—one carries a metal axe—but there is no gratuitous violence or murder until Aton arrives. Even in a Hell much like Dante's, Aton is the source of evil.

At the opposite extreme, in the paradise of Idyllia, Aton attempts to overcome his minion heritage and love Coquina. But at the critical moment, he imagines her as a minionette and pushes her off a cliff. During his final battle with Chthon's representative, Aton struggles to reconcile these opposing sides within himself and finally accepts himself for what he is, resolving his guilt. He returns to Coquina purged of his desires for Malice and of the guilt he had hidden from even himself for raping his mother. He makes his final peace with himself before he can make peace with Chthon and accept a compromise: he willingly returns to Chthon in exchange for Chthon's promise to preserve Coquina from the fatal disease—the Chill—she has contracted.

The series of myths in *Chthon* defines Aton's conflicts and helps him to overcome them. The Oedipus sequence creates his guilt and his urgings. The Dantesque suggestions of Chthon as Hell, Idyllia as Paradise, make possible his release from the Hell of himself, just as he escapes from the physical hell of Chthon.

In *Phthor*, the mythology works on much the same basis. Classical and Christian references, however, diminish and are replaced by a more powerful set of figures: the Norse gods and their irrevocable movement toward Ragnarok. In the "Interlog" of *Phthor*, Anthony makes the transition explicit:

> Arlo retreated to the world of LOE [*Literature of Old Earth*, his present on his seventh birthday], the garden of his mind. He shied away from the Oedipus/Electra mythologies, seeking something less painful, yet applicable. A framework for his situation, buried in the massed Human wisdom of the book . . . .
> And found himself in Norseland.

Most of the key figures in Norse mythology are represented: Aton, now one-eyed and wielding an axe, is equated with Odin; wily, deceitful Bedside becomes the Loki-analogue; Aton rides on an eight-legged beast named Sleipnir, after Odin's Horse; Aton's first son, Aesir (one of the two divisions of gods in Norse mythology, whose joining with the Vanir resulted in the birth of Odin and his fellow-gods), was killed by Bedside in a manner recalling the death of Baldur. Three half-zombies, the only survivors of the Hard Trek of *Chthon* besides Aton, survived by merging with Chthon to become the quasi-prophetic Norns: Verthandi, Urdur and Skuld. And Arlo eventually manifests as Thor, complete with gloves, hammer, and a "belt of strength."

As Thor, Arlo organizes the war against Chthon on the basis of the mythology—and mythology ceases to be mere legend and becomes a tool for shaping the present and the future. Arlo convinces Chthon that he is thinking in mythic patterns; yet Arlo's inversions of the roles of myth and reality reveal myth as ultimate reality. The battle in the world-encircling caverns of Chthon becomes a literal Ragnarok. Chthon has allied himself with other mineral intellects throughout the galaxies; and their Chill, which has ravaged sentient life, is merely the precursor of the ultimate kill-chill, a wave sent by the mineral intellects to initiate interactions between oxygen and fluorine and destroy all life, opening the way for further mineral development. Arlo sees visions of the two possible ends of the conflict; the victory of Life, which results in sentient forms warring against each other in their efforts to despoil and exploit the planets; and the victory of Death, in which all life is destroyed.

Arlo tries to forestall either alternatives, realizing that Ragnarok—the conflict between Good and Evil, between Life and Death—is itself the evil. The sides are not good or evil in themselves. Arlo-Thor attempts to stop the battles, extending his mental control outward and halting individual fighting. But at the critical moment, he is threatened by Chthon's greatest monster, an immense dragon, the analogue of the Midgard Serpent who destroyed Thor. Arlo can battle the Serpent, but to do so, he must release his control over Ragnarok. He is denied the possibility of compromise, and the conclusion of the novel is predicated on Arlo's final choice.

The mythologies embedded in *Chthon* and *Phthor* go far beyond mere ornamentation or surface symbolism. They define the thematic content of the novels. Initially, there is a clear demarcation between myth and reality. Young Aton knows firmly who he is and what his destiny will be. He also knows what myths and legends are—they are the stories contained in his birthday present, the thick volume of *Literature of Old Earth* that he carries with him throughout his early life and finally abandons in Chthon. Yet early in *Chthon* Anthony throws that clear demarcation into question. To Aton, minionettes had always been myths—like nymphs and sirens. Yet suddenly, terrifyingly, he discovers that they are real. By the end of *Chthon*, *Literature of Old Earth* lies deserted in the darkness and Aton has embraced the realities underlying the myths.

In *Phthor*, Arlo relies on his understanding of myth, until he realizes that his own life is a re-creation of a complex derived from an amalgam of myths. He understands the relationship of myth to his own life: "The caverns have taken the place of capital punishment," Bedside tells him. "There is no release; it is like the mythic underworld" (Ch. I). As Arlo works through the forms of the mythology, however, he moves beyond their literary and symbolic value, and the myths become literalized. In the final episodes of the novel, he penetrates mythology, freeing his mind until he becomes not merely a character playing out the mythic roles assigned him, but an apotheosis, a god. Arlo's enhanced animate mind grapples with Chthon's mineral intellect. The result of their interaction is as explosive as the interaction of oxygen and fluorine threatened by the kill-chill.

Anthony's emphasis on myth as structure leads to his theme in both novels—control. In *Chthon,* the control required was internal. Like so many of Anthony's characters, Aton is an arrested juvenile during much of the novel, struggling to define himself, his desires, and his responsibilities. He initially fails. But when he is imprisoned in Chthon, he gradually develops the self-control necessary to integrate both his minion and his human heritages by means of compromise, rather than through simplistic choices between right and wrong, good and evil. Finally, he returns willingly to the caverns, to live under the dominion of the mineral intellect; Chthon, in turn, promises to preserve Coquina from the killing effects of the chill. As long as both parties keep their agreements, there is peace.

In *Phthor*, the need for control and compromise expands to include not only Aton and his family, but the entire galaxy and its four forms of sentience. Arlo's visions quickly convince him that neither the forces of Life nor the forces of Death can be allowed victory; both must be controlled and directed to forestall galactic chaos. Toward the end of the novel, Arlo neatly recapitulates Anthony's thesis in these two novels, and in much else that he has written:

> "You are assuming that I am opposed to Chthon." Torment's knife whipped around—and stopped as his mind clapped down on hers.
>
> "I'm on the side of sanity," Arlo said, letting her go. "I don't mean to destroy Chthon. Chthon is not evil—it is merely a different way. We have to work out a compromise for mutual survival. Each side has things the other side needs. Life has mobility, technology, reproductive capacity—the ability to change the physical aspect of the galaxy and to adapt itself to what cannot be changed. Chthon has—proportion."
>
> ". . . Unchecked, Life will destroy itself and the galaxy . . . . Some control needs to be exercised. Chthon is that

33

control. Together, in harmony, the two will make of this realm a paradise—for both'' (Ch. VII).

Should Chthon prove victorious, all life would disappear from the Galaxy; but the prospects should Life win are equally bleak:

> Throughout the galaxy the species of Life are warring. Human fights over some trumped-up charge of planet rustling; EeoO fights Xest over the price of the Taphid, which happens to originate on an EeoO planet. The resources of whole stellar systems are being wastefully depleted. Once the sentience of Chthon was destroyed, no one seemed to care about mineral values (Ch. VI).

At the end of this second vision,

> Arlo woke sweating with revulsion and horror. *The vision of Life's ascendency was as bleak as that of Chthon's.* Each victory meant awful death for those closest to him, in that microcosm reflecting the carnage of the macrocosm . . . .''The essence is this: we cannot afford Ragnarok. Our victory is as bad as Chthon's. *No matter who wins, Evil prevails.* Compromise is essential'' (Ch. VII).

This is the threat of the Blast that predates the shattered cultures of *Battle Circle*, the Blast that in this case threatens galaxy-wide obliteration of all life forms.

Unfortunately, Arlo discovers this too late; Chthon is already implacably dedicated to the war and refuses offers of compromise. Arlo cannot convince him/it of the need for an integration of the powers of Life and Death, of the necessity that the dually-destructive Y-figure be reformed into "the I-course of a single, successful future" (Ch. VII). Arlo, and his hope, are destroyed in the shattering conclusion of his struggle, as the interaction between Arlo and Chthon signals the apotheosis of sentient and mineral intellect:

> Desperately, Arlo tried to demolish the structures [controlling Chthon's kill-chill circuits] before his own mind collapsed. As desperately, Chthon sought to trigger it off, though the guiding chill-wave had not yet arrived. As a result, it changed. It drew into itself in a kind of short circuit all the reserve powers of Chthon, coalescing about very special, potent substances, merging oxygen and fluorine in an entirely new and thorough manner, not restricted to organic material but all-inclusive, tapping violently into it without the limiting fuse of Arlo's brain, resulting in—
> Phthor (Ch. VII).

In the Epilog, *Phthor* is defined: a quasar, a galaxy-wide explosion. Yet, as in *Battle Circle*, there is hope, even in the ruins following the Blast. The survivors—the remaining mineral intellects—finally understand what Chthon did not, and they now commit themselves to a third course of action: compromise. From defeat and destruction comes the possibility of a coherent, controlled civilization.

In addition to the overriding theme of control, Anthony also develops several secondary themes. One is Anthony's conviction of the unity of life, defined most clearly in the passages detailing the intimate relationship between humans and the Hvee, a semi-telepathic plant that flourishes only in an ambience of love and trust established with a single individual (*CH*, Ch. I). Similarly, Anthony's aliens—startling and imaginative, as his creations typically are—do not differ in motivation or concern substantially from the humans they are intended to measure. Even the mineral intellects share human motivations by the end of the novels.

Inversion plays a prominent part in the novels, as is typical of Anthony. The minionettes are inversely telepathic: they perceive pain as pleasure and pleasure as pain. In fact, they can be killed only by overt expressions of love. Aton shares this inversion; Arlo shares it to a more limited degree and transcends it. And throughout the novels, Anthony consciously inverts the readers's expectations. In the prison caverns, nudity becomes as neutral as clothing, while clothing becomes titillating (an inversion that will appear again in *Split Infinity* and *Blue Adept*). Struggle is the key to true joy. Reality is revealed as no more relevant than myth, while myth in turn becomes the key to understanding reality. Since sanity destroys in the prison caverns, insanity alone survives the tortures of Chthon. And, of course, there is the apparent inversion of Chthon and Idyllia, opposites located on the same planet.

Another characteristic of Anthony's writing showcased here is his delight in punning and word games. In both *Chthon* and *Phthor*, names are often multiple puns revealing not only the character's literal function in the novel (Ma Skinny, a portly woman, is so named because she hands out water skins to new prisoners; Chessy carves chess sets from garnets) but also their symbolical or metaphorical roles. Aton, "child of the sun," is restricted from the sun forever, to dwell in the darkness of the caverns. Arlo takes on the name of Phthor, a conflation of Thor and Phthor (which Anthony identifies as an old name for fluorine). Arlo is both god and element of destruction, and his name so indicates. Names also become the basis for verbal games (another favorite device of Anthony's). Aton Five's name, for example, can be translated into itself mathematically (*CH*, Ch. II). This emphasis on names and naming is not accidental. To name is to know and control. Over and over, characters refuse to divulge their true names, since if they do, the hearers know who they are, what they did, and how they can be controlled.

And finally, Anthony again works with the theme of sterility/fertility. Children are essential in Anthony's worldview; it is part of the tragedy of *Battle Circle* that main characters are incapable of bearing children or that children die young. The same is true of *Chthon* and *Phthor*. The prison caverns are sterile; no births take place save those allowed—or manipulated—by Chthon. Arlo is the only one to survive in the caverns, and he dies childless. Aton fathers three children, each playing an essential role in the final battle, but none surviving to bear children. The cataclysm at the end of *Phthor* suggests a possible future, but there are no children. At this point, there is only barrenness.

Chthon and *Phthor* are intriguing novels with much to offer a reader willing to concentrate on them. *Chthon* is self-consciously mythopoeic in tone; *Phthor* is somewhat more realistic, partially because of Anthony's interest in the development of adolescent sexuality in the later volume. The novels are complex, convoluted, inverted—and powerful. In incorporating the multiple strands of technique and theme and in intertwining them with pre-existent strands of mythology, Anthony has himself created an enduring and a moving myth.

NOTES:

1. Biggers, p. 57.
2. *Publishers Weekly*, 22 May 1967, p. 180.
3. Leo Harris, *Books and Bookmen*, April 1970, pp. 26-27. The key here is the phrase "and, after a while, understanding." *Chthon* is not an easy novel to work through, but it richly repays the effort.

V

THE OMNIVORE SERIES

1. *Omnivore*

Omnivore, the first novel of a trilogy centering around the inter-planetary exploits of a team of three explorers, is an overtly didactic work and shares both the strengths and weaknesses of didacticism. The main character—or at least the one present through most of the novel—is Subble, a physically and mentally modified government agent assigned to interview three explorers—Veg, Aquilon, and Cal—and through his investigations to discover both the problem he was sent to solve and its solution. Yet Subble is in many ways merely the ostensible hero; the trio is more central to the novel and lead to Subble's own confrontation with the alien life forms he must understand or destroy. And the trio more clearly define Anthony's underlying concerns in the trilogy; Subble remains largely peripheral to them.

Omnivore does not follow a straight-line narrative; in this respect, it reflects Anthony's interests in time-manipulation developed in *Chthon* and *Phthor*. The novel is divided into four sections, representing encounters between Subble and the explorers and between Subble and the alien mantas. Within each section, there is a split time differential; the novel begins with Subble interviewing the characters (or battling the mantas, in part four), then, shifts to the past to re-create a portion of the team's experiences on the manta's home planet, Nacre. An early review referred to the plot of the novel as "as tightly woven and as suspenseful as that of a detective story," [1] and indeed Anthony develops it as a detective story. With each encounter, Subble (and the reader) learns a bit more about the team's adventures and comes one step closer to unraveling the mysteries surrounding the trio. And with the final meeting be-tween Subble and the mantas, the reader discovers the most dangerous secret of all, a secret which, in good science-fiction fashion, threatens to destroy all life on Earth. The novel ends with what is at best a stop-gap conclusion and a preparation for the sequel.

Within the framework of this detective story, however, Anthony creates a far more complicated web of themes and interests. Leo Harris commented that *Omnivore*

> could almost be a Western. Indeed, it started off in a Mid-West logging forest somewhere North of Appalachia, where an isolated community lives a simple life. To them comes Subble, basically a human frame, but stripped down and souped up so that he (and other detectives like him) can be ruthless, logical and incorruptible in their search for truth. Chesterton would surely have approved. Further, his masters have *not told him what his mission is* so that his mind is free from all possible preconceptions. The contrast between the simple fist-fighting loggers and the subtle Subble is piquant, and Subble's adventures as he strives to save Earth from the threat of a life form that is more dangerous dead than alive, are varied and violent. [2]

Harris' review is misleading for a number of reasons, the most important being that it places too much emphasis on Subble as super-detective and entirely de-emphasizes the individual episodes surrounding Veg, Aquilon, and Cal. It ignores entirely Anthony's explicit concerns in *Omnivore*, mirrored in the title of the novel. Like *Battle Circle*, *Chthon* and *Phthor*, *Omnivore* deals with control—specifically, with controlling the most dangerous omnivore of all, man. Throughout, Anthony dichotemizes order and disorder, control and lack of control, understanding and ignorance, and their accompanying results, power and powerlessness. On an Earth that is rushing toward the Blast that set the stage for *Battle Circle*, the characters must unravel the mysteries of order and control, first among themselves, then in the ecology of Nacre, and finally between Nacre and Earth.

The three explorers represent brawn, beauty, and brains in their own classification. Chapter I, "A Loaf of Bread," introduces the brawny Vachel Smith, nicknamed Veg. His confrontation with Subble is physical and includes a ritual fight reminiscent of *Battle Circle*, with accepted and proscribed punches, a circle defining the battleground, rigid rules for participation, and an absolute lack of animosity among participants outside of the circle. During the battle royal, Subble earns Veg's respect as a fighter, and consequently, Veg relates the first third of the team's experiences on Nacre: their introduction to the mantas and their almost disastrous attempt to assert physical superiority over the alien life-forms.

Aquilon is the beauty of the trio but hides from the pressures and complexities of Earth by refusing to smile (just as Veg had retreated into complete vegetarianism). Her meeting with Subble is more sophisticated but similarly results in his winning her confidence and hearing her portion of the tale. In the process, Anthony re-introduces an important theme in the novel—man's inhumanity as omnivore. Aquilon's tale also moves the narrative forward another third, to their discovery of the omnivore of Nacre. The three humans parallel the evolutionary development on Nacre: Veg is vegetarian, an herbivore, in essence and by choice; Aquilon is an omnivore; and Cal is a carnivore, capable of living only on human blood. In a moment of crisis, Veg and Aquilon offer Cal their blood. The action unifies the trio, salving over an incipient break resulting from sexual tensions. Just as an omnivore devours both herbivore and carnivore, Aquilon stood between the two men, loving both, yet unable to decide between them or to fully understand the relationship between them.

The third chapter, "A Book of Verses," represents the intellectual contest between Cal and Subble, structured around Cal's discovery of the three kingdoms of life on Earth: animal, plant, and fungus—the latter living on the decay of the two former and essential to their survival. Through a series of visions that are unusually ingenious and vivid, Cal convinces Subble of the danger to Earth's ecology should the relationship between plant, animal, and fungus be altered. Then he leaves the agent, forcing him to seek a resolution among the mantas themselves.

The final chapter, "Wilderness," blends the main themes of the first three. Subble is isolated with the six mantas on an island near the Florida coast. He must understand them sufficiently to comprehend the threat they pose to Earth and then either subdue or destroy them. The battle again reminds one of the ritualized warfare of *Battle Circle*: the six aliens surround Subble; then, one moves in toward him. For the first time, Subble discovers the nature of his adversaries. The manta is virtually unstoppable—yet it must be stopped. Subble realizes that

> Man and manta had won their respective places by becoming the most deadly fighters of their worlds. The order of precedence had to be established before higher negotiations could begin. This was the essence of natural selection; not pretty, but necessary (Ch. IV).

Subble wins, although the victory kills him. And out of respect for him and because of their acquiescence to his higher physical and mental status, the mantas relay to government headquarters the report Subble would have made and thereby condemn themselves.

The key here is that the nearly unlimited power possessed by the mantas and Subble is valuable only when it is controlled, as defined by physical and mental strength. As the mantas perceive it,

> the omnivore had proven itself. It had risen above the terrible limitations of its physique to meet a civilized creature on even terms. Now at last it was permissible to converse with it without restraint, while Pent dissolved into smoky spore vapors. The other omnivores had been innocuous pets, un-

able ever to comprehend the code of the warrior, unworthy to share the information of the elite. This one—this one was contemporary (Ch. IV).

Anthony approaches a potentially distasteful stance: might makes right. Yet given the circumstances he creates for Earth, there is little other choice. Her crowded billions are increasingly neurotic. The three explorers have diverted their neuroses into peculiar directions: Veg into vegetarianism, his personal response to death; Aquilon into her obsession that her smile is horrific (she takes the one feature that had given others pleasure when she was a child and twists it into a grimace and a parody); and Cal into his delusion that he can subsist only on human blood, an inverted death wish denied only when to fulfill it would require the sacrifice of Veg or Aquilon. Subble alone is without such neurotic obsessions—significantly so because he is without any conscious past. He, like all agents, has had all memories and all individuality excised. One of the "SUB" series of agents, he is less than human; yet he alone has the strength to counter the threat the mantas represent.

In such a world, control is necessary. Humanity is constitutionally incapable of regulating itself. As omnivore, man destroys other life forms, as well as himself, as is mirrored in Cal's vampirism. The mantas define Earth as

a wilderness world without true order; the life forms were far more vigorous and tenacious than those they had known. But Subble had approached sentience, and his kind deserved a chance (Ch. IV).

Surgically altered and modified, only he is capable of doing so, and the novel ends with that hint of hope.

It should be noted that Anthony's inclusion of vegetarianism is more than merely a literary curiosity. Much as in the nearly contemporary "In the Barn," Omnivore is an overt plea for respect for all life—human and animal. Anthony's sympathies are clearly defined throughout the novel—perhaps too clearly defined. And to the extent that this didactic concern intrudes itself, characterization and plotting are potentially weakened. The three humans and Subble succeed, as long as they are allowed to grow into invidiuals. Veg, Aquilon, and Cal, however, threaten on occasion to degenerate into stereotypes: Cal, for example, is the thin, intellectual scientist about to lose the beautiful girl to the muscular but naive sidekick. Only when his addiction to blood becomes known does he break from the stereotype. And the same is true of the other characters. Subble has difficulty rising from the level of 007 super-agent, but eventually even he begins to come alive.

On the other hand, Anthony's imagination is at its best in the creation of Nacre and the alien mantas:

The mushroom world of Nacre is original and cleverly constructed, with well-developed systems of botany, biology, and ecology; but the fanciful science backgrounds don't intrude on the plot. [3]

The more one discovers about the mantas, the more they capture the reader's attention. The reader begins to think of them as merely mantas, i.e., as a recognizably terrestrial form; even Subble makes that nearly fatal mistake. But ultimately, the mantas defy being faint reflections of Earthly reality. They become powerful symbols as themselves. Anthony allows them to exist as truly alien.

Omnivore intrigues on a number of levels and fails on others. The manipulation of time and the gradual revelation of mysteries are well handled and impel the reader forward. The mantas, omnivores, and herbivores of Nacre are original, exotic, and stimulating. Yet there are difficulties with the novel, as two reviewers who so casually classified it as "western" or "detective" suggest. Some elements are overstated and tend to obscure Anthony's larger purpose. Neither reviewer seems aware of Anthony's use of over-crowding as a metaphor for human societal problems, of vegetarianism and its concommitant awareness of the right to life at all levels, of the difficulties of controlling the omnivore's more obvious destructive tendencies, and of the human being as ultimate omnivore. In spite of the dangers of falling into momentary stereotypes, however, *Omnivore* remains a challenging novel.

2. *Orn*

To refer to the sequel, *Orn*, as "one of the best man and dinosaur yarns, and a little more" [4] is to approach one of the main strengths of *Orn*, but just as certainly to mislead and misdirect. The novel contains its share of adventure, including an extended man versus dinosaur episode, the stakes being control of an alternate earth. But *Orn*, like *Omnivore*, aspires to being more than a mere "yarn." The "man and dinosaur yarn" continues the process of defining the nature of the omnivore—of man.

The narrative begins with the nascent memories of the title character, Orn, a large, flightless, sentient bird, the apex of avian evolution on the Earth-alternate, Paleo. Orn's intelligence is of an entirely different nature than man's, and for this reason the initial chapter of the novel is difficult to follow. Fluctuations in time and space are confusing until the reader is told that "racial memory was [Orn's] instrument of survival—a device like none ever employed by another species" (Ch. 1).

Interspersed with Orn's odyssey to discover a homeland and a mate, the narration begun in *Omnivore* continues. Veg, Aquilon, Cal, and the four remaining mantas are transported to an alternate Earth, ostensibly to report on the flora and fauna of Paleo (so named because of its resemblance to Earth 65 million years ago). During their survey, the trio discovers an enclave of saurians in a single volcanic valley. And eventually their path crosses that of Orn and his mate Ornette, forcing interaction between the two intelligent species.

Orn is from the beginning more technical than was *Omnivore*. Much of the novel is devoted to discussions of evolution, geological epochs, geology, zoology, biology, and paleontology, [5] but in spite of momentary hesitations, Anthony presses on with the themes begun in *Omnivore*: the nature of the omnivore, the over-crowding of Earth, the relationship between life and death, and the proper means of establishing control.

Nacre, inhabited by fungoids, was essentially alien; Paleo, on the other hand, is an alternate Earth. The human intruders must face a reflection of Earth's own past and share a world with two other survival-types, the avian Orn and the Saurian Tyrann. The humans effect brief relationships with their fellow creatures. Veg and Aquilon swim to Orn's island, where they are allowed to land. After examining them and listening to the sounds of their lovemaking, Orn decides that the "giant mams" are helpless and have come to him for protection. Even though he is an omnivore, he accepts them. Later, during an earthquake, Aquilon saves Orn's egg and carries it through the rest of the novel. Orn and Ornette eventually sacrifice themselves to save Aquilon and the egg; Anthony hints that a close relationship between alien species, even between omnivores, is possible.

Cal, on the other hand, attempts to create a similar interface with the saurians. Determined to report Paleo as an ideal outlet for Earth's crowded populations, he decides that there must first be a test. He, as mam (mammal), represents the apex of one evolutionary line, Tyrann (tyrannosaurus rex) another. Cal explains to the mantas that Tyrann's

> world is on trial. If I get to the radio and send my report, my people will come and exterminate the biological system that now obtains. Not all at once, but over the years, the centuries, until the only dinosaurs remaining are caged in zoos, and the same for most of the primitive Paleocene fauna. Modern mammals will be introduced that will compete aggressively with the less sophisticated natives, and the trees will be cut for timber and pulp and the rocks mined for precious minerals. So *Tyrannosaurus* is fighting for his world, though he doesn't see it that way. If the reptile brings me down, the report will not be made, and man will not come here—at least, not quite so soon. If I escape the reptile, I will have vindicated my fight, according to the implacable law of nature, to supersede it on *Paleo*. It is a contest between us, and the prize is the world (Ch. 14).

Cal establishes a primitive "battle circle" and contracts to abide by the outcome of that conflict. Anthony pits the physical might of Tyrann against the intellectual might of Cal in an hours-long battle. At dusk, above the snow line, Cal finds a volcanic cave and hides in it, leaving Tyrann to prowl outside. The drop in temperature during the night assures victory for the man; Tyrann's blood is incapable of retaining the heat necessary for his immense bulk. By morning, he is cold, nearly lifeless.

Cal thus wins the right to make his report. However, he wins an even more important battle—a battle with himself as a member of an omnivorous species. He chooses not to leave Tyrann to die. Instead, he stimulates the saurian, kicking and yelling at the beast. Though lethargic, Tyrann rises and stumbles slowly down toward the plain. Cal has established his superiority on Paleo through trial by conflict with the saurian champion. His decision, however, is atypical for an omnivore; he decides for life rather than for death, allowing Tyrann to live out his time on Paleo rather than polluting the alternate-Earth with the spillover from a neurotic and destructive Earth. He decides *not* to report. *Orn*, then, seems more optimistic than *Omnivore* had been. The trio represents the human race, omnivores by species. Cal, the most urgent in pressing for Earth's perquisites, compromises with himself, with Paleo, and with Tyrann, allowing each to survive.

But government agents interfere, agents more advanced than Subble had been. As Cal walks toward the plains, moments ahead of the sluggish saurian, he suddenly sees a human figure:

> "Veg!" he cried. But it wasn't Veg.
> The man nodded briefly, hands on his steam rifle. "Dr. Potter, I presume."
> The exchange had taken five seconds. It was enough of a pause to bring Tyrann into sight. Still clumsy but recovering nicely, the dinosaur bellowed and charged down at them. Almost casually, the stranger aimed his weapon and fired. A hiss as the steam boosted away the shell and dissipated; a clap of noise as the projectile exploded. As Cal turned, Tyrann began to fall. His head was a red mass (Ch. 19).

At the last moment the true omnivore reveals himself—the agent. Tyrann dies, a victim of Earth's ambition and desires.

Similarly, Ornette dies trying to protect her eggs from an omnivorous Plesiosaurus. Orn is killed attacking an agent to protect Aquilon and the egg. Two mantas suicide, releasing fertile spores throughout the valley and potentially destroying Paleo as a haven for humans. And then the agents reassert their essential natures by callously burning the entire dinosaur enclave. Anthony carefully and graphically describes the death-throes of the saurians . . . in nauseating detail, through the eyes of Veg, Cal, and Aquilon. He is purposefully brutal [6] to convince the reader of man's ultimate responsibility for the torture and pain inflicted upon the dinosaurs. Through the trio, the reader is forced to participate in the omnivore's exploitative destruction of the enclave. Aquilon and Veg accept the futility of their entire experience in Paleo:

> The dream of bliss was cruelly ended. The idyll of Paleo had been revealed as genocidal naivete. What good was it now to feel sorry for Elas, the one-time enemy plesiosaur? It was less vicious than man.
> She had known it before. She had seen this on earth, this savagery (Ch. 22).

Cal alone realizes the importance of Paleo:

> The enclave was nothing. Paleo was nothing—nothing more than the convenient battleground. There would be a million enclaves, a billion Paleos, and trillions, quadrillions, quintillions of *other alternate worlds*. This was what the confirmation of the parallel-worlds system meant . . . . No alternate world could match Earth *exactly*. No two alternates could jibe precisely for that would be a paradox of identity. But they could come close, *had* to come close—and Paleo and Earth were close . . . (Ch. 22).

Cal understands the threat of the omnivore. Man had already shown himself incapable of co-existing with the alien intelligence of the mantas and the now-dead Orn. But even more disastrously, he had shown himself incapable of co-existing with a close alternate to his own world. And now that Earth had discovered the existence of the alternate frames, it would attempt to conquer and destroy, all in the name of human-kind. Cal alone knows this at the end of *Orn*; the working out of the implied threat is reserved for the final volume, *OX*.

Orn is in fact an idyll separating the more didactic novels, *Omnivore* and *OX*. It is more devoted to action and adventure than was the first novel; it includes multiple encounters with strange beasts and savage creatures, narrated from the humans' and the avians' points of view. *Orn* seems more concerned with story than with elucidating a theme—even Veg's vegetarianism is down-played substantially.

Still *Orn* remains uneven. Schuyler Miller argues against Anthony's use of Latin contractions—e.g., *mams* for mammals, *reps* for reptiles, *Arky* for Archelon (prehistoric turtle)—particularly against their use by Orn, a Paleocene bird with no functioning language. [7] And the constant use of the abbreviation does occasionally draw attention to itself, especially when humans with no contact with each other decide independently to use the same abbreviation to designate a particular animal. But in a larger sense, the use is characteristic of Anthony's delight in language. It becomes a kind of game, creating from the full word a shorter form that is at once a pun (Tyrann is indeed tyrannical, and the "'Quilon mam'' is a ma'am) and an evocation of the most important elements of that creature's make-up.

A more precise and justifiable complaint against the novel is Greg Bear's:

> There are times when Piers Anthony is a frustrating—in fact, maddening—author, very confusing. *Orn*, for all its quality of imagination and use of unusual themes, fails for me because of the woodenness of its characters and the sporadic quality of its writing. I've reached that dubious point where 'acceptable' writing quality leaves me cold. While Anthony's scope and imagination in *Macroscope* swept me away and the flaws be damned, *Orn* . . . doesn't do that. [8]

There are indeed times when the characters cease being individuals and become representatives of types or species. There is no indication, for example, that any members of Orn's species exist, other than Orn and Ornette. As a result, they become more emblematic than individual, just as Veg is quintessentially the vegetarian man of peace who can be riled enough to become very destructive or Aquilon is the typical woman caught between her desire for a strong, physically appealing man, and a physically weak but intellectually powerful one.

One must also add the constant diversions into geology, paleontology, and a host of other sciences dictated by Anthony's choice of time and setting. In fact, the novel concludes with a Postscript by Calvin Potter, nothing less than a disquisition on the mysterious extinction of the dinosaurs. These technical digressions are not without interest, but they frequently clash with an otherwise active plot and sweeping narrative, creating an unevenness of texture and development that occasionally irritates.

3. OX

The third volume of the trilogy is more complex than the other two and reflects Anthony's interest in time and space first explored in *Macroscope* and later to form the framework of the Cluster novels. In *OX*, Anthony continues to define the omnivore by placing the trio—accompanied by mantas, the fledgling Ornet, and extra-human agents Tamme and Taler—in contact with a variety of alien races on alternate frames. Of the aliens, the sparkle-clouds and the sentient machines are the most critical.

OX is not easy, superficial reading. As one reviewer noted,

> A dense texture of cross-purposes, ambiguities of time and space, and the gradually manifest presence of a sentient super-computer make this a book for readers willing to put

This is a fair assessment of the novel; unlike *Omnivore* and *Orn*, whose narratives continued essentially intact, in spite of shifting time-frames and points of view, *OX* consists entirely of manipulations of time and space, incorporating sparkle-cloud-entities capable of aging sentients at will by passing them through alternate frames. To increase the complication, Anthony does not define or describe his aliens and their abilities; the reader discovers the aliens, just as the characters do. The first chapter, "Trio," introduces the narrative by having Veg suddenly materialize onto a desert world—apparently another Earth-alternate—and immediately have to fight off an omnivorous machine. He flees into the desert. Aquilon appears, still carrying Orn's egg, sur- veys the damage done to their supplies, and sees Veg's tracks leading into the desert. As she considers what to do, a naked woman materiali- zes, demanding the egg. Aquilon recognizes the woman as an alternate Aquilon but refuses to relinquish Orn's egg. In the ensuing struggle, the egg is crushed, and the alternate Aquilon disappears. Then Cal comes through, sees both the ravaged supplies and the distraught Aquilon, and the two set out after Veg. They are in turn set upon by a sparkle-cloud and whisked away to yet a third alternate world.

Then Anthony introduces Ox, a sparkle-cloud creature, a pattern crea- ture only recently sentient and aware only of a single directive: survive. And finally, the agent Tamme follows the trio from Paleo. She tracks Veg, the machine, Cal, Aquilon, and the mantas until their trails di- verge; then she follows Veg's and finds him in the desert. They too are captured by a sparkle-entity and transported to the intermediate world.

With this basic cast of characters, Anthony creates a series of conver- ging narratives. Cal and Aquilon remain in the City to communicate with the sparkle-entities. Veg and Tamme enter projectors to attempt a re- turn to Paleo, Earth, or the desert-alternate and instead find them- selves on a closed-loop of alternates, following and fighting alternate Vegs and Tammes. OX, in the meantime, gradually identifies the three "spots" within this complex of patterns as Cub, an infant human, born of Calvin Potter and an alternate-Aquilon; Ornet, hatched from the egg preserved by an alternate Aquilon; and Dec, an infant manta pulled from the same frame. The four entities develop awareness of each other and of themselves: OX first and most fully, then Ornet with his racial memory. Cub remains dependent and helpless, with Dec, Ornet, and OX protecting him. Then, an infant machine intrudes into the com- plex, ravaging and destroying. In one frame, he slices up the human infant. Cub is saved when OX throws out a temporal shoot and moves in- to another time-space frame, in which the machine is decoyed away.

Anthony uses complexities of plotting and development to further his definition of man as Omnivore. Cal, Veg, and Aquilon unitedly oppose the omnivorous agents and the governments so represented. They divide their responsibilities: Cal and Aquilon try to communicate with the sparkle-entities, while Veg projects with the agent Tamme into the alternate worlds. Anthony's love of games is emphasized again. The series of worlds is arranged as a hexaflexagon—twelve worlds connected in precise patterns. As Veg and Tamme work their way through the game worlds, she gradually recovers the memories erased during the process of becoming an agent. In a climactic encounter on the alternate world Bazaar, attended by a multitude of alternate Vegs and Tammes and Cals and Aquilons, Tamme fully accepts herself for what she is:

> We represent the natural selection of that fragment of the circuit that met their doubles—and lost, so were delayed for recovery. Out of all the other possibilities happening elsewhere. So we know first hand: We are omnivores, destroying even ourselves. Yet it seems that the male-female aspect enhanced the chances for survival as though something more than mere competence were operant. We may have redeeming qualities (Ch. 15).

Aware of their natures, the alternate normals and agents decide not to report any of the alternate Earths, since that would merely result in attempts from *each* Earth to destroy its counterparts and move unrestricted into the potentials of "alternity," the billions of other Earths existing seconds from each other. However, since none can return to their original Earths, they return instead to their points of entry in the alternate-frame and await the pleasure of the sparkle-entity responsible for placing them there initially.

All of this leads up to one of Anthony's perennial themes, the interdependence and unity of all life. Interlinked with an Earth computer, OX defines himself as

> the code designation of Zero X, or Arabic numeral nothing multiplied by the Roman numeral ten, themselves symbols for frame-representations that cannot be expressed in your mathematics. Zero time ten is nothing in a single frame, and dissimilar systems can not interact meaningfully; but in the larger framework the result is both infinite and meaningful, expressing sentiences . . . (Ch. 16);

That larger framework is explored in the chapter entitled "Report," as Anthony defines the underlying experimental structure of OX's enclave:

> Pattern-entities, unable to comprehend the nature of physical sentience, but unable to ignore it as a potential nonsurvival threat, instituted an enclave consisting of five divergent sentient entities—a pattern, a machine, and three forms of

life— fungoid, avian, and mammal (Ch. 18).

Since the enclave was designed to test the interactions of sentiences, it did not include sufficient nutriments for life, thus directly stimulating competition for survival among the five. In addition, the pattern entities created the hexaflexagon worlds and transported mature specimens of sentient species there, allowing them to observe some of the interactions within the enclave and with the multiple worlds of alternity.

The experiment failed since the entities within the enclave survived in spite of their competition—in fact, they cooperated to ensure mutual survival. The experimenters lost interest and failed to establish further communication with the enclave entities or with the alternate humans and agents chasing each other through the twelve test worlds. Consequently, the experiment endured for considerably longer than originally intended, until the entities in the enclave developed "complete and free interaction."

> We—the five sentient entities of the enclave—have worked out the principles of such interaction . . . . We feel that the fundamental knowledge must be placed in the minds of those entities best able to utilize it, with the provision that it be used only to facilitate harmony and progress among all the alternatives. We feel that four of our five representative species lack suitable philosophies or talents for this purpose. The fungoids and the aves do not have either the inclination or the manual dexterity to operate the necessary constructs. The mams have both—but lack appropriate social control. They are predators, exploiters: in their own description, "omnivores," destroyers of differing systems. Therefore this power cannot be entrusted to their possession. The pattern-entities are also capable and have better philosophical mores. But their cynicism in setting up this enclave and the associated 'hexaflexagon' pattern of alternate frames shows that their philosophy is incomplete. Sentiences are not to be toyed with in this fashion . . . . Only one species possesses incentive, capability, and philosophy to make proper use of the information and to carry through effectively on the implied commitment. For this species only, we append our technical report granting the power of alternity.
> We believe the machines well serve the need (Ch. 18).

OX is the logical culmination of patterns developed throughout the trilogy—and through Anthony's novels. Since human beings are incapable of monitoring themselves, they require external control. Omnivore ends with the ominous image of an atomic blast; Orn ends in destruction by fire. OX finally suggests a mode by which this innate destructiveness might be contained. Even though the machines are initially described as ravagers, devourers, within the enclave the infant machine Mach follows rules that gradually develop limits to their counterattacks. Just as the four other sentients struggled to survive, so Mach attacked solely because he craved minerals their bodies contained; indeed, he fought off the urges to attack as long as was "machinely" possible and consistently refused to follow up any advantages his attacks gave him. Mach proved himself superior—morally, intellectually, and physically—and in doing so gained for himself and his kind control of "alternity."

In *Omnivore*, relationships are largely among the initial trio: Cal, the carnivore; Veg, the herbivore; and Aquilon, the omnivore. In *Orn* the struggle broadens, to include the dimension of alternate frames. In *OX*, whole species are tested, grow, and mature sufficiently to recognize their inabilities. In that sense, the trilogy is a realistic appraisal of man's potential. Anthony refuses the easy solution of a human race that miraculously grows and matures within the limits of a few pages. Neither, however, does he retreat into pessimism and adumbrations of disaster, as Walter Miller does in the conclusion of *A Canticle for Leibowitz*. Instead, Anthony assesses the human race, finds it lacking in certain essential areas, and then devises a structure by which it might be guided in its progress. The external control is not debilitating; opposition stimulates strength. Cub realizes, as does OX, that without the threat represented by Mach, the enclave entities would not have interacted for their mutual survival. So Anthony's solution, while idiosynchratic, is not simplistic or superficial.

Though occasionally uneven, the trilogy is exciting in scope and power. It moves through time and space, entering a universe controlled by games which finally reflect a larger reality. The characters are occasionally wooden or stereotyped; but at the same time, Anthony allows full play to his imagination, peopling the alternate worlds with a peculiar array of aliens who are indeed *alien*. *Omnivore*, *Orn*, and *OX* are partially marred by their didacticism, but they nonetheless repay a close reading.

NOTES:

1. *Publishers Weekly*, 11 November 1968, p. 52.
2. *Books and Bookmen*, July 1969, pp. 38, 46.
3. *Publishers Weekly*, p. 52.
4. Schuyler Miller, *Analog*, June 1972, p. 171.
5. This point is discussed in the review in *Publishers Weekly*, 3 May 1971, p. 58.
6. Anthony consciously uses brutality as a means of communicating in his stories and novels; in this respect, see "On the Uses of Torture," (*The Berkeley Showcase, Vol. 3*, ed. Victoria Schochet and John Silbersack [New York: Berkeley, 1981], pp. 80-101. Of this story Anthony says:

I wrote it a decade ago but could not get it published, until today my increasing reputation makes it possible to place the same piece. I suspect it is the most brutal SF ever done (Letter, June 7, 1980).

The editors of the *Berkeley Showcase* agree:

> The following story is one of the most revolting we've read. It is exploitative, bludgeoning, and completely, utterly compelling (p. 79).

The brutality is purposeful in Anthony: man is a brutal creature, and often such measures alone can shake him from his course of action.

7. Miller, p. 172.
8. Greg Bear, *Luna Monthly*, October/November 1972, p. 36.
9. *Publishers Weekly*, 26 July 1976, p. 78.

VI

MACROSCOPE

Macroscope is one of Anthony's most ambitious and complex novels, an ingenious combination of hard sciences—biology, astronomy, physics, paleontology—with history, music, and astrology. It continues and completes a number of Anthony's persistent thematic concerns, including the need for maturity and control. But *Macroscope* moves beyond the other novels to suggest man's place in the galactic scheme and the galaxy's place in a larger order. It is, in Samuel Mines' words, "A stunning *tour de force*":

> *Macroscope* recaptures the tremendous glamour and excitement of science fiction, pounding the reader into submission with the sheer weight of its ideas which seem to pour out in an inexhaustible flood . . . . The effect is one of opening up the mind to tremendous new horizons, to see worlds one never dreamed of and to struggle with concepts that enlarge the universe to frightening dimensions . . . . *Macroscope* is an impressive piece of work and is not to be missed by anyone who enjoys science fiction. [1]

The novel can be divided into four sections: the Macroscope (Ch. 1-4); the escape to Neptune (Ch. 5-7); the Destroyer (Ch. 8-9); and the astrological/symbolical assessment of man's role in the galaxy (Ch. 10). The sections begin firmly in the reader's objective world, then gradually develop both spatially and metaphorically to extend beyond the limits of the physical galaxy and beyond the limits of man's imagination.

The first section, the Macroscope, suggests a detective story. There are two mysteries: (1) the nature of the macroscope and (2) the identity and location of the mysterious Schön, ostensibly the only person capable of solving the first—and most critical—riddle. The main characters are introduced: Ivo Archer, with his double-pun name; Brad Carpenter, an amoral genius whose 200-plus I.Q. is exceeded only by the elusive (and even more amoral) Schön's; Afra Glynn Summerfield; Harold and Beatryx Groton, an engineer and his uniquely normal wife; and Schön, whose presence is felt throughout the section, even though he never appears.

The plot revolves around the discovery of the macroscope, a device for uniting Earth with the galaxy surrounding it. The macroscope transmits images stored on macrons, either contemporary images or reflections of galactic history extending back thousands of years. From the space station, an observer using the macroscope could literally see anything happening on Earth (from reading secret documents sealed in a safe to participating in voyeuristic adventures in bedrooms) or watch the decline of sentient civilizations dead thousands of years. Through the transmissions, scientists discover that most cultures, upon reaching a particular technological level, tend to destroy themselves internally through overpopulation, pollution and exploitation of natural resources, and finally through ritual cannibalism—problems which Anthony points out already exist on Earth and characterize the society of the mid- to late-1960's.

But there is a problem with transmissions. Among them is one—the Destroyer beam—which bars access to other transmissions and burns out the brains of viewers intelligent enough to understand it. Five top scientists have been reduced to near vegetables. And thus the introduction of Ivo Archer to the plot.

Archer is a near-normal, with slightly above-average intelligence and two exceptional talents—music and an ability to play mathematical games, such as "sprouts," a game that becomes critical to the plot toward the end of the first section. In spite of his normality, he is forced through a "cloak-and-dagger" episode to come to the station. The opening section is largely devoted to Carpenter's attempts to convince Archer to summon Schön, the only human capable of resolving the riddle of the Destroyer.

In the process, Anthony gradually unfolds the intricate details of the macroscope's construction, functioning, and dangers, while simultaneously bringing up a number of social issues he feels are critical to human survival: birth control, elimination of pollution and apathy, release from the pressures of over-crowding. In addition, he increases the frequent punning characteristic of *Macroscope*; nothing, it seems, means explicitly what it says. Characters' names, their patterns of speech, their phraseology—all are consistently revealed to contain multiple meanings, each meaning appropriate to a stage of development within the novel. This is particularly relevant with Archer, Carpenter, and the unseen Schön (the multiple meanings of his name are discussed frequently by other characters).

The crisis of the Destroyer beam is heightened by the arrival of an ambitious, intelligent, and skeptical Senator, who demands to view the beam—and is destroyed. Brad Carpenter is also brain-burned. The political complications underlying the functioning of the station are such that the Senator's death will trigger movements to dismantle the macroscope. And without Carpenter, the mind behind its construction, there seems little hope to salvage the project before a United Nations fleet arrives. At this point, Afra and Harold take charge. Archer is forced to enter a "sprouts" tournament; his intuitive grasp of games allows him to win the championship, a curiously shaped trophy (with a touch of Anthony's scatological humor, as well as an implicit assessment of the role of the macroscope), and the right to the macroscope. The tournament—nothing less than a trial for control by ritual battle, reflective of both *Battle Circle* and *Orn*—is a mental game, rather than a physical confrontation, but the principle remains the same. Archer proves himself superior to his competitors and, accompanied by Afra, Harold, Beatryx, and the damaged Carpenter, he steals the macroscope and blasts away from the station.

The novel narrows its focus tremendously at this point: from Archer as one among millions of average Americans to Archer as one of hundreds in the station to Archer as one of four functioning representatives of the human race entrusted with the secrets of the macroscope. Toward the end of the section, Anthony makes clear the relationship between the macroscope and the four humans:

> The Doctrine of Microcosm and Macrocosm—that is, the concept of the individual as the cosmos in miniature, while the greater universe is total man in his real being.

Although it is not yet obvious, this is precisely what *Macroscope* is concerned with—the relationships between the individual, the human race, the galaxy, and the cosmos. Peter Brigg defines the novel as

> comprised of a series of intricately interlocked sequences integrating the scientific and humanistic ways of presenting the doctrine of microcosm and macrocosm, of showing that the pattern of the unity of all things can be traced in the subatomic particle, in man or in the stars.   This doctrine is actually a statement that the entire universe is related in terms of the analogies of scale. [2]

By the end of the first section, Anthony has introduced his characters and the major complications of plot. These chapters are generally straightforward, with little manipulation of time or space (except for passages, narrated by Archer, that seem to be taking place in the South of the Civil War). The four characters are isolated on a ship, heading away from Earth; yet Archer is still speaking of Schön as someone they could conceivably contact. And the menace of the Destroyer beam has not been alleviated in any way.

The second section details the escape from the station to Neptune. The fugitives are in danger; a robot United Nations ship has been dispatched to apprehend them and return the macroscope. Laden as they are—and organic as they are—they cannot attain the velocity necessary to escape a robot ship, nor can they allow the macroscope to be retaken and dismantled. Archer manages to penetrate the Destroyer and, by doing so, opens thousands of new channels. He discovers a way to outrun the ship and reach Neptune—their goal, since a cryptic punning message from Schön has directed them to go there.

The method of travel is critical to Anthony's thematic purposes in the novel and is both inventive and original. It entails

> "No freezing, no tanks," Ivo said. "No fancy equipment. All it takes is a little time and a clean basin."
> Afra looked at him suspiciously, but did not comment.
> "What are you going to do—melt us down?" Groton.
> "Yes."
> "That was intended to be humorous, son."
> "It's still the truth. We'll all have to melt down into protoplasm" (Ch. 5).

The process requires that they relinquish their essential identity, return to a primal state, and then reconstitute. Afra is particularly terrified of the procedure; she feels the need for some security that the person reconstituted is in fact herself. She demands a "Handling":

> "She is trying to preserve her identity," Groton said helpfully. "But it isn't an entirely physical thing. She requires an *experience*—emotional, sexual, spiritual—the words are hardly important."
> "Sexual?" The inane query was out before [Ivo] could halt it.
> "Not stimulation in the erotic sense," Groton replied carefully. "It is possible to copulate without any genuine involvement, after all. Rather, a shared sensation. Your actions and reactions are an important part of it, for they deepen its relevance. When you interact with intimacy, you accomplish something meaningful. She does not exist alone; she needs an audience. Otherwise, like the unread book or the unheard symphony, she is unrealized. Move her, be moved by her; make an experience whose significance will not easily fade. *React!*" (Ch. 5).

Afra's fears help explain Anthony's frequent use of juvenile sexual discovery as the focal point of plots. Sex—for Afra, as well as for other characters, including Arlo (*Chthon*) and Dor (*Castle Roogna*)—is a means of establishing identity and definition. She uses the Handlings as a means of fully preserving her sense of self.

The melting is important in another way. Ivo supervises Afra's melting—and Anthony describes it in minute, often horrific detail. The horror helps define what it is to be human: what bodies are like, how they function, and how closely identity is tied to the body.

When Archer reconstitutes Beatryx, her organism recapitulates evolution, from cellular structure to fish, to reptile, to mammal, and finally to primate. Near the end of the process, Anthony describes the thirty-seven year old Beatryx: "Goddess of fertility, she lay upon her back and contemplated him through half-lidden eyes" (Ch. 5). Then the aging continues and Beatryx emerges superficially identical to her former self—but only superficially. The melt-down and reconstitution metaphorically suggest that the four are not quite the same as their earlier manifestations. They are now in orbit around Neptune; they belong only marginally to the society of Earth, even though they do not quite recognize that fact. They move increasingly away from that society as they tap into the advanced technology of the macroscope transmissions to find means to survive on Triton, the largest of Neptune's moons.

Over the months, they grow in subtle ways, altering in their actions and their personalities. Ivo reveals more about his past, a past shared with Carpenter and Schön. He is the result of a project intended to determine whether intelligence could be achieved through breeding. The project developed only two geniuses, Carpenter and Schön. Its ultimate failure lay in the children's isolation from others of their species. From this point on, Anthony emphasizes the importance of relationships in developing maturity within a species, or among species. Schön, the product of ultimate isolation, is immature and totally amoral. Ivo could contact him, but fears to, understanding the extent to which Schön is a monster.

While on Neptune, the four solve yet another mystery—Harold Groton casts horoscopes for each member of the expedition. In doing so, he discovers that Ivo Archer could not possibly exist—and that the data Archer had supplied him with fits closely the horoscope of Sidney Lanier, a nineteenth-century poet. Confronted with Groton's findings, Ivo admits that he *is* Schön. Archer is an alter-ego invented by the genius when Schön was only five. Maturing without a past, Archer retained his humanity by building on the life-history of Lanier, partially because of Lanier's abilities as a flautist. Archer alone can call up Schön from the depths of his mind, and he refuses to do so because of Schön's self-obsessive ego.

Eventually Ivo discovers a means by which the group can track down the source of the Destroyer beam, in essence, a mode of interstellar (if not intergalactic) travel. He defines a second channel, dubbed the Traveler beam, through which physical structures are reduced to gas. The entire entity is then compressed beyond its own gravitational limit and punches its way into another section of the galaxy. Using Neptune as a stabilizing mass, Ivo initiates the process by which the team can travel beyond the Solar System. Speaking of Anthony's style, relevant to this final passage of the second section, Brigg states:

> . . . Anthony employs his writing skill to produce passages of
> particular resonace, lyrical "purple passages" inserted like
> small reflective gems in a golden setting to reflect the
> strength of the concepts of unification and the power of
> macronic technology. The description of the harnessing of
> the macronic technology in order to move Neptune in such a
> passage, carefully building to an explosive burst of action and
> ending with the simple yet spectacular statement: "Man's
> physical exploration of the cosmos had begun." [3]

Brigg disagrees—at least as far as this sentence is concerned—with the
general sense that Anthony's writing does not match the level attained
by his imagination and his ideas. Yet Brigg is correct in this case; the
single sentence is simple, yet spectacular.

In the third section, the quartet sets out to discover and destroy the
source of the Destroyer beam, the single impediment to humanity's
conquest of interstellar space. Anthony begins to depend more and
more upon animations through the macroscope, rather than on the
straightforward experiences of the characters. Through this means, he
reveals that the difficulties faced by modern man—pollution, corrup-
tion, over-crowding, fear, ignorance—are not unique to our century.
In essence, Anthony argues, humans as a species are too immature to
develop a viable, desirable civilization on a galactic level. The more
Archer delves into the mysteries of the macroscope, the more overtly
Anthony makes his points, and simultaneously, the closer the amoral
Schon comes to the surface of Archer's mind.

During the course of their explorations, the four humans accidentally
penetrate the limits of the galaxy itself. They no longer receive controlled macronic transmission; instead, they tune in on "wild macrons"
that have circled the galaxy for millions of years. They see segments
from the origins of the galaxy, from the development of life on Earth
until the rise of mammals. Much of the description reflects Anthony's
interest in geology and paleontology, given full play in *Orn*.

Finally, however, they arrive at the source of the Destroyer, a heavily
armed space station. The armaments, curiously, have been turned off,
and the explorers enter. They discover an atmosphere attuned to
humans, and earth-like gravitation. And strangest of all, the interior
is a museum, whose exhibits gradually evolve into tests of the obser-
vers' intelligence, creativity, and maturity. One by one, the group
solves the challenges, opening a series of rooms, until they arrive at a
room with a single artifact—a musical instrument. Ivo plays it but does
not play music as such. Instead, he plays a poem, Lanier's "The
Symphony," an attempt to bridge the realms of poetry and music.
And with the beginning of the poetry, amplified by Afra's analytical
mind, Harold's astrological symbology, and Beatryx's human/maternal
empathy, the novel moves into the fourth, and most problematical
section.

In the Biggers interview, Anthony specifically stated that many of his readers were upset with the astrological element in *Macroscope*. [4] Mines sees it as an unfortunate digression in an otherwise masterful novel. [5] Brigg, on the other hand, argues persuasively that the astrology is essential to the development of *Macroscope*, since it provides patterning to Anthony's ideas.

> The astrological symbols occur again in "The Symphony" Ivo plays, whose movements are divided by the primary signs of the characters: Schön in Aries, Beatryx in Pisces, Harold in Libra, and Afra in Capricorn. In following his sign each character lives out an experience which is part fantasy, part event. Then Afra and Schön struggle for survival in a contest set in the context of astrological houses. . . .Schön nearly defeats Afra because he understands symbolic patterns such as the horoscope. Astrological symbols are vital to the novel because they bind the human and physical universes, providing a symbolic pattern which makes all events comprehensible. [6]

The animation-visions allow Anthony to explore human potential in light of what he presents as Galactic history: a series of civilizations that achieve interstellar travel too soon, through the mediation of the Traveler beam, and consequently destroy each other in uncontrolled wars of conquest. Beatryx and Harold form the center of two such animations and are lost because of their inability to withstand either temptations or pressures. Only Afra and Schön/Ivo survive with the potential to become one with the unity that Anthony sees as underlying the galaxy. In the final struggle, Afra wins, largely because she recognizes the Traveler beam for what it is: a sentient being.

> Originally it had evolved from mundane forms, but its technology and maturity had enabled it to achieve this unforeseeable level, freeing it of any restraint except the limitation of the velocity of radiation through space. Even that could be circumvented by using the jumpspace technique—once space had been cartographically explored by lightspeed outriders.
>
> There was nowhere in the universe this species could not range.
>
> But very few life-forms ever achieved this level. Why? The Travelers investigated and discovered that in the confined vicious caldron that was the average life-bearing galaxy, the first species to achieve gaseous-state jumpspace capacity acted to suppress all others—then stagnated for lack of stimulus. The problem was that technology exceeded maturity. Only if more species could be encouraged to achieve true maturity could universal civilization become a

fact. They needed time—time to grow. And so the Travelers
became missionaries (Ch. 10).

The Destroyer beam becomes, with a typical Anthony inversion, pro-
tective rather than destructive; it effectively blocked species not yet
capable of handling advanced technology from receiving the Traveler
channel. And the Traveler, which had been viewed through much of
Macroscope as entirely beneficial, is shown to be incipiently destructive for any species or civilization insufficiently mature to handle itself.
As happens in many Anthony novels, ostensible friends are unmasked
as enemies, and obvious enemies are revealed as benefactors.

Here the breadth of *Macroscope* is fully developed. Anthony's quest
is for maturity essential to progress, but not the maturity of an individual, or even a species (as in *Battle Circle* and the Omnivore series):

> *Species* might suffer, but *galaxies* were prodded into growth.
> Those galaxies that achieved control over their immature
> elements—so strikingly defined by their actions in the face
> of jumpspace temptation—were on their way to success.
> The Milky Way, after several failures, had finally gained that
> self-control, and was on the verge of full maturity—as an
> entity. This was the gift of the Traveler: the passport to the
> universe, and to universal civilization (Ch. 10).

This awareness provides Afra with the information she needs to
reverse Schön's string of victories in the astrological animation contest.
Then Anthony reveals the final mystery of Schön's disappearance into
the innocuous personality of Ivo Archer—and why he was unable to
emerge without Archer's permission. It is in some ways a weakness in
the novel that this key information is withheld until the final chapter.
In detective novel parlance, the author is hiding essential clues from
everyone except his detective. And the result is the same; Afra's victory is lessened and the conclusion of the novel weakened.

But Anthony manages to overcome this flaw as he ties together the
threads that have interwoven throughout the novel. Man is integrated
and matured: on a galactic level, by achieving parity with other species
that merit knowledge of the Traveler, and on an individual level, as
Ivo-Schön merges the strongest elements of his separate personalities
and matures into a new humanity. Again, the characters are not entirely
successful, but they are usually convincing, particularly Afra's renun-
ciation of the immature but brilliant Schön and of the mature but self-
limiting Archer.

> But the destroyer had shifted the balance and broken the
> stalemate making Ivo the artist. He could unify and control—
> and time and experience had made his identity the more fit
> of the two for human intercourse. A child normally grew into

an adult—and to abolish the adult Ivo in favor of the child Schön would be a foolhardy inequity.

Thus the personal equation. Boy had not won girl; man had won woman (Ch. 10).

Ivo Archer's personal victory parallels the entire set of analogous victories, encompassing the microcosm and the macrocosm, that are the interest of *Macroscope*.

Macroscope is a powerful novel, if somewhat over-long. A plot summary must of necessity do injustice to the individual elements of the work. As is usual with Anthony, he is more concerned with definition of key thematic interest than in plot; and in cases of possible opposition between the two (as in the incorporation of the astrological vision-animations), he will choose the former. And as is equally usual in Anthony, *Macroscope* becomes a testing ground for several essential problems: control, maturity, and discipline on an individual, social, planetary, and galactic scale. He defines the new species of human beings required to claim their rights as part of galactic society—and equally defines their responsibilities. He incorporates a number of devices into the narrative, including intricate inversions of nature and reality; literary allusions that gradually take on the force of reality; games and puns that parallel his social concerns and punctuate them; and an increasing use of typographical experimentation to augment the printed passages. Throughout, he emphasizes the possibility of man's joining with other species in a larger universe, a theme he will develop and investigate even further in the subsequent Cluster series.

NOTES:

1. *Luna Monthly*, September 1970, p. 22.
2. "Analogies of Scale in Piers Anthony's *Macroscope*," *Science-Fiction Studies*, 2 (1975), p. 125. Brigg's article is one of the few critical studies of Anthony's works.
3. Brigg, p. 129.
4. Biggers, p. 61.
5. Mines, p. 22.
6. Brigg, p. 125.

VII

AURAS AND ANIMATIONS

1. The Cluster Trilogy

In the Cluster trilogy, Anthony continues his interest in galactic adventure: *Cluster* recounts the conclusion of the First War of Energy between the Milky Way and Andromeda; *Chaining the Lady* moves forward a thousand years to the Second War of Energy; and in *Kirlian Quest*, Herald the Healer, a member of Sphere / of Andromeda, marshals the combined species of both galaxies to combat an invader from beyond the galactic cluster—the space amoeba.

In rough outline, the books suggest the most blatant of space opera: alien invaders (physical and mental); swash-buckling adventures, complete with heroic one-on-one battles and exotic weapons; nubile females; and more than a liberal sprinkling of sex (although most of it is alien). The tendency toward space opera was recognized by Gerald Jonas when he commented that in *Cluster*,

> Anthony has avoided the problem of late-chapter letdown by writing what appears to be a series of opening chapters. His hero, Flint, comes from a stone-age planet . . . he learns how races with three sexes make love, and other important facts of life. This space opera with panache never takes itself too seriously, even when the fate of the universe is at stake. [1]

What Jonas says about one applies to all three. Throughout the series, Anthony seems to be enjoying unabashedly the thrill of creativity and imagination, peopling his galaxies with a host of truly alien beings, and taking delight in defining their alienness for the reader. More than anything, the Cluster series is an exercise in enjoyment.

In many ways, however, it is unfair to dismiss the trilogy as merely "space opera with panache." As in his other novels, Anthony deals with serious themes, while at the same time incorporating irrepressible verbal and situational humor. Among the more intriguing elements that go to make up the series are his use of the Kirlian aura; his use of the

Tarot; and his constant references to analogies between the mythological world of constellations and legends and the realities experienced by his characters. According to *The Readers Guide to Science Fiction*,

> Weaving with words is an apt analogy for his *Cluster Series*, a magnificent tapestry with inter-galactic war and fascinating speculation on development in the use of Kirlian auras merely the basic fabric. Set in this background are carefully picked out threads of thoughtful creation; detailed sexual, emotional, and societal examinations of various alien and humanoid species that compose the membership of the Milky Way and Andromeda galaxies, romantic interludes between friends and/or enemies, and a complex and rational use of Tarot cards and readings. [3]

Among Anthony's innovations in the series, his incorporation of the Kirlian auras is the most intriguing. The auras are of paramount importance in the trilogy, since they facilitate communication between species, making possible galactic and inter-galactic civilization. In this respect, the Cluster series is like much of contemporary science fiction—concerned with problems of communication and the structures which make that communication possible.

Cluster introduces Kirlian transfer, by which the aura of one entity is transferred instantaneously into the body of any other galactic entity. At the beginning of *Cluster*, instantaneous inter-stellar traffic is limited to "mattermission" and is cripplingly expensive in terms of energy required; Anthony had already explored the devastating effects of such an energy drain on a society in *But What of Earth?* Consequently, inter-stellar travel of items larger than a gram or two is limited to ships, with the obvious result that fringe regressions take place. Flint of Outworld, a native of a planet circling Etamin, lives at a stone-age level, near the outer limits of Sphere Sol.

When an alien envoy from Sphere Knyfh offers Sphere Sol the secret of Kirlian transfer on the single condition that the Solarians spread the technology among their neighboring spheres, as a means of solidifying the Milky Way against the encroachment of Andromedan agents and their attempts to bleed the Milky Way of its essential energy, the Solarian authorities ("Imps," as Flint calls them) draft Flint as their prime agent. His Kirlian aura is two-hundred times human normal, and the only difficulty with Kirlian transfer is that the transferred aura fades by one unit for each day it is separated from its natural body. Hence the importance of using high-Kirlian entities as agents.

Convinced that he must help his galaxy, Flint embarks upon a series of episodic adventures among entities of Canopus, Spica, Capella, Polaris, and finally a jaunt in his own body to a newly discovered ancient site in the Hyades. This final exploration is of particular importance, since the Ancients—known only through their ruins scattered throughout the galaxies—were apparently Super-Kirlian entities, and their technology is essential to continued galactic civilization.

Flint succeeds in forestalling Andromeda's invasion of the Milky Way, but fails to uncover the more critical secrets of the Ancients, including the technique of hostaging a host against its will. The Andromedans, however, make this discovery a thousand years later and initiate the Second War of Energy in *Chaining the Lady*. In this volume, Melody of Mintaka (Kirlian aura 215) must discover the extent to which the Milky Way has been infiltrated by Andromedan Agents in hostage hosts. The primary action of the novel centers on the Milky Way fleet, a collection of some hundred ships from the galactic spheres. The fleet has been ravaged by hostaging. Using her Tarot cards, Melody identifies the hostage aboard the flagship and provides the catalyst for a premature Andromedan attack. In true space-opera fashion, Melody finds herself with a handful of allies, pitted against the combined might of galaxy Andromeda. There is action sufficient for any enthusiast: individual combat, duels, betrayals and counterbetrayals, and a climactic battle, in which the forces of the Milky Way are outnumbered two to one, and Melody suddenly becomes the Admiral of the galactic forces.

But the Milky Way loses and Melody is transferred to Andromeda where, through a series of accidents and devious elusions, she activates an Ancient site, discovers a devastating secret about the Ancients, and is transferred back to her own galaxy just before the site detonates. Thus the Second War of Energy ends. In her final seconds of consciousness at the Ancient site, she reverses all hostaging, making it impossible for an alien aura to inhabit a host without permission. She returns to the Milky Way, to find the Andromedans captives of the hosts they had originally invaded, and the Milky Way is victorious after all. She refuses to disclose what she has learned about the Ancients and dies, taking the secret with her.

Kirlian Quest recounts the adventures of Herald the Healer, of Sphere/ in Andromeda. His Kirlian aura is 236, the highest recorded in galactic history. Another thousand years have passed, and now the galactic cluster—composed of the Milky Way, Andromeda, Pinwheel, and several smaller stellar globules—is threatened by an external force, the Space Amoeba. Only high Kirlians can counter the attack—or even identify it—so Herald becomes involved in more episodic adventures, each leading him closer to the secret of the Ancients, and to a confrontation with the Amoebites. During the course of his adventures, he meets, marries, and loses Psyche, whose aura varies from a respectable twenty-five to an incredible 350, when amplified by a functioning Ancient site. His experiences culminate with the final confrontation with the Amoebites, and the resolution of the three-thousand year old galactic conflict for energy.

Throughout the trilogy, and in *Thousandstar* and *Viscous Circle* [4], Anthony makes ingenious use of the Kirlian aura as a structural device. Each novel explores a facet of Kirlian transfer, the reader discovering its potentialities as the characters unravel them. [5] *Cluster* describes the initial aural transfer among Solarians, with the accompanying problem of adaptation to alien cultures and body-structures. *Chaining the Lady* defines the crisis of identity that hosting—particularly involuntary hosting—entails. And *Kirlian Quest* examines the healing uses of aura as Herald literally heals on multiple levels: Psyche, himself, his sphere, and his galaxy. He uses aura to resolve the conflict with the Amoebites but without resorting to violence. Only in *Thousandstar* does Anthony break his own rules concerning Kirlian transfer. Transfer is only possible among entities of the same or compatible sexes. This rule is so absolute that transfer becomes a mode for defining sex among multi-sexed species. Yet, through an intricate (perhaps too intricate) series of occurrences, the key transfer in *Thousandstar* results in a female aura co-habitating a male body. Most of the novel is taken up with dialogue between the two—with some interesting speculations concerning male and female psychology, motivation, and needs.

A second feature of the series is Anthony's use of the Tarot. He is aware of the atypical structural modes in his novels. In an interview, he noted that

> Those (readers) who didn't like the astrology in *Macroscope* will be apoplectic at the Tarot theme of *God of Tarot*. [6]

The comment is appropriate here, since the Tarot motif is first developed in *Cluster*, then applied full-cloth in the Planet of Tarot series.

As is usual with Anthony, he is not content merely to borrow a structure; he must alter it to make it unique to him. The Tarot is no exception. His *Cluster* Tarot is composed of five suits (including, appropriately enough, a suit of *aura*) and one hundred cards. [7] The Tarot is also divorced from mystical, fortune-telling functions. Instead, it clarifies information already present in the character's mind. As Hugh Pendexer has defined the Tarot in Anthony, with particular reference to *Flint of Outworld*:

> He leaves the reading with a new sense of purpose and direction, not because the cards have revealed the future, but because they have helped him clarify his own perception of past and present, thus also clarifying his perception of his mission and the probable success of various lines of action . . . . Thus throughout the *Cluster* trilogy, the Tarot pack works psychologically, not mystically, to unveil only the postulant's own conclusions. [8]

individuals are associated with the particular cards, as a means of identifying their potentials, and species are likewise associated with one of the five suits. The battleships of various entities are in fact constructed to reflect the Tarot suits affiliated with the species: as a thrust-culture, the Solarians build ships resembling swords, while the water-dwelling Spicans build cups and the magnetic Knyfhs build atoms.

Tarot functions, much as did the astrological references in *Macroscope*, to define human characteristics, strengths and weaknesses and to relate them to the macrocosm. The Tarot binds all sapient entities in the Cluster, providing a single symbolic system for communications and understanding. And, not coincidentally, it provides Anthony with a unifying thread for the six novels that define his super-galactic civilization.

Analogy between microcosm and macrocosm plays a role in the Cluster series, although on a slightly different level than in *Macroscope*. In *Cluster*, entities are identified by name and planet/star/galaxy; i.e., Flint of Outworld (planet), Melody of Mintaka (star), Slash of Andromeda (galaxy). This designation is nearly constant: only Herald the Healer is referred to by function rather than place of origin. Chapter titles similarly suggest placement in the galaxies; in *Cluster*, "Ear of Wheat" takes place on Spica, and "Tail of the Small Bear" on Polaris. This sense of analogy and placement is important in two ways. First it allows Anthony to define characters. Reference to Polarians, or Spicans, or Canopans automatically defines their idiosyncracies (perhaps one of the flaws in Anthony's imagination is that he frequently allows a single entity to represent an entire galactic sapience). But even more importantly, it defines the essential character of the inhabitants of that area, by analogy with the constellations involved and the mythology developed to describe that constellation. As Flint of Outworld notes on his initial visit to Capella:

> There was no Charioteer constellation, of course, because Capella was *in* it, as the eye of Auriga, mythological inventor of the chariot. The colonies were well aware of the places of their systems in human mythology, and Flint had no doubt the chariot was an important symbol here, just as the dragon was around Etamin (*CL*, Ch. 6, "Eye of the Charioteer").

Chaining the Lady expands the sense of analogical relationship to include galaxies. It develops the myth of Andromeda, as the title indicates, with Melody of Mintaka variously taking the roles of chained lady and monster. Throughout, Anthony uses images of construction, of patterns intersected and inverted, and of external threat to one's identity. In the end, Melody is "chained" as her Mintakan body and her host's body are forced into sexual expression, changing her from female to male and thoroughly altering her sense of self.

This use of analogy connects closely with the Tarot—the one a means of symbolically expressing perceptions and awarenessnes, the other a means of relating those perceptions to the larger universe. As the Epilogue to *Cluster* states,

In Galaxy Andromeda, Melody was honored in his female form, represented in the Queen of Energy or Thirteen of Wands card of Tarot. But it was mooted privately that the name of the lovely chained lady was Andromeda, as the Solarian mythology had said all along, and that the name of the sea monster was Melody.

And no higher compliment can be paid a sapient than that paid by the Polarian Tsopi to Flint of Outworld: "You have reenacted the legend of your star" (*CL*, Ch. 7).

Both the Tarot and the astronomical analogies are essential to the series because they define the individual and his place in the microcosm. This, of course, has immediate relevance to Anthony's continuing theme, most fully developed in *Kirlian Quest*, of "Soul sapience," his obsession for species maturity from *Macroscope* presented in a different imaginative framework. Yet the result is the same. Entities capable of meeting the challenge of mattermission and Kirlian transfer without succumbing to the temptation of conquest and devastation (and in *Kirlian Quest*, this includes nearly all sapient species in the galactic cluster) are ready for the next evolution of civilization. Where in *Macroscope* Anthony introduces the attenuated Traveler beam entity, he here creates the Ancients, whose mission is to discover and preserve species who show potential (closely related to Kirlian aura) for soul sapience. Herald the Healer provides an archetype for this development. Initially, he is competent as both heraldic scholar and healer (hence his double-pun name) but immature, overly concerned with the disgrace of his species during the Second War of Energy. He was confident in his Kirlian powers, but in little else. He is self-negating, self-abrogating; he finds it impossible to believe that the beautiful Psyche of Kade could indeed love him, or that he could love her for more than her fluctuating aura.

Gradually, through the episodes of the novel, he matures sufficiently to sacrifice all he possesses—including Psyche, not accidentally named "Soul"—to serve the greater demands of galaxy and cluster. In doing so, he gains in understanding and maturity and is able to avoid violence in meeting the threat of the Amoebites. He sees life as it is, not as generations of sapients had imagined it to be. As he says to the Amoebite commander:

> . . . we are mutually guilty. *We* were looking for super-Kirlians, so did not recognize you when you came. *You* were looking for weed-species, so did not recognize the fruit of your prior effort here. We *both* saw you as conquerers, exterminators, so of course you were. But now we can work together to solve the problem we both face. Energy. (*KQ*, Ch. 12).

65

At this point, Anthony concludes the trilogy. It is a fascinating series of adventures, characterized by unfailing inventiveness both in plot and characerization, in description and in typographical innovation. If anything, the novels suffer from a surfeit of inventiveness—after a while, the astounding ceases to astound. The trilogy is an important work, for Anthony as a writer [9] and for the reader. It is more approachable than *Macroscope*, broader in its exploration of space (although not of time), while bearing much the same sort of thematic weight. It is less didactic than many of the earlier novels, integrating message with adventure and plot, and combining the whole with a sense of pure enjoyment of intellectual exercise, puzzles, puns, and typographical experiments. Anthony uses the trilogy to examine relationships between human capacities, supported by an intriguing admixture of Tarot and astronomy, of science and mythology.

2. Planet of Tarot

Perhaps the best way of summing up the impact of the Cluster trilogy is to look at in the light of the subsequent series. The final paragraph of *Kirlian Quest* reads:

> So the Kirlian Quest was ended in the Cluster—and initiated in the Universe. The figure of Herald the Healer, savior of the cluster, became a part of history, joining those of Melody of Mintaka and Flint of Outworld. Only one more story remained to be told: that of the last—more correctly, *first*—of the shapers. This was the founder of the Temple of Tarot, whose amazing private experience provided the philosophical grounding for all that followed. He was brother Paul, an obscure novice in an obscure sect of pre-Spherical Planet Earth during its Fool period. His was the quest for the God of Tarot.

Brother Paul had appeared briefly during one episode in the Cluster trilogy and had a fairly major role in the earlier *But What of Earth?* but his story is fully told in the Tarot trilogy: *God of Tarot*, *Vision of Tarot*, and *Faith of Tarot*.

Anthony assessed the trilogy as both his most important and most controversial work. [10] He had good reasons for considering it so. As it stands, the trilogy takes as its overt subject the definition of God not in an exclusively theological or philosophical sense, but according to the hard evidence of science as modulated by Tarot animations and recorded by Brother Paul of the Holy Order of Vision during his mission to the planet Tarot. "If I succeed," Anthony has said, "*God of Tarot* will eclipse *Macroscope* as a novel I am known by. The fans may not like it, because it isn't what they expect from me, but I'm aiming for a larger audience." [11]

Unfortunately, he seems not to have succeeded as well as he hoped. The trilogy is in some ways a throw-back to the structural patterns of *Battle Circle*. It is a repetition of the brutality and horror of that world-view, without the redeeming vision of a new civilization to be produced from present turmoil. The Tarot series is blatantly offensive, through its constant scatological themes and images, its consciously perverted sexual references, and its attitudes toward religion. Perhaps more to the point, however, it combines brutality, horror, and disgust (none of them foreign to Anthony's novels) with a curious tediousness of action. Most of the trilogy takes place during animations controlled by the Tarot and ranges from near-autobiography (Anthony's visit to Vermont as a participant in a Science Fiction panel is closely detailed in *God of Tarot*) to fantastical visions of Satan and Hell. But somehow, Anthony's imagination does not succeed in welding the pieces together; the episodes become drawn-out, confusing, and on occasion rather boring. The series is atypical of Anthony in many ways, and not particularly an improvement in either technique or narrative ability.

Like most of his novels, however, it is complexly organized, with a number of disparate strands, each leading to a partial definition of God. The novels each relate to the Tarot. The planet on which they take place is named Tarot. Paul's visions of his own past, of the history of religions, and of Hell, are all stimulated, frequently controlled, and almost always most easily interpreted by the Tarot cards he holds. Structurally, the Tarot organizes the entire trilogy around the triumphs beginning with the Fool and ending with Triumph 28, Completion (*FT*, Ch. 9). In each chapter, the action centers around the characteristic defined by the controlling triumph.

The Tarot is linked with a second phenomenon—the animations. They are so intimately related that on Planet Tarot they merge, to create the Animation Tarot, an instrument for knowing that develops into the Cluster Tarot of the Cluster series. The Tarot series (particularly volume III) provides insight into the function of Tarot in the cluster novels by defining not only the historical Tarot, from the middle ages through the twentieth century, but also the future Tarot of Brother Paul. The combination of Tarot and Animation allows high Kirlian sentients to project visions perceivable by others. These are not hallucinations nor the results of mass hypnosis; instead, the Animation invests reality with an overlayering that can be controlled by the mind in charge. Through the Animation, the individual may learn important lessons about himself, his preconceptions and prejudices, and—in Brother Paul's case—the past, present, future, and the natures of God and Satan.

However, as Brother Paul soon discovers, before he can approach Satan, he must first understand himself. In the final chapter of *God of Tarot*, he remembers an incident from his past that defines his—and by extension, man's—nature:

> He smelled shit. And he knew. This was the Animation that
> revealed his inner worth, the sources of his feculence. . . . He
> had murdered an innocent girl, ten years ago. Or nine, or
> eight. Mnem [a memory-enhancing drug that destroys
> memory when it is withdrawn] had shrouded his memory,
> and now Animation had brought it back, his dirtiest secret.
> He was worthless (*GT*, Ch. 8).

There is a hint of optimism in the judgment; as Brother John responds, "Fecal matter is the raw material for compost, a vital stage in the cycle of renewal . . . . There must be death and rebirth and between them is the soil" (*GT*, Ch. 8). But the conclusion of the novel remains unreasonably depressing and rather more simplistic than is usual in Anthony's fiction.

Much the same might be said for the remaining two novels. In *Vision of Tarot*, Brother Paul investigates the history of religions in an effort to isolate the religion which best defines God. Having come to an awareness of his own worth, he realizes that he cannot know God by himself, so he approaches the problem obliquely, through the evidences of history. Like John Milton in *Paradise Lost*, he has no further confidence in the abilities of self-willed individualistic warriors, as he had tried to be in the first volume. And he realizes that no individual can make full sense of an animation, so he proposes an alternative. In the company of several citizens of Planet Tarot—including a devil worshipper, a Mormon, and the requisite nubile beauty—he suggests an Odyssey through time, via Animation, to examine the roots of various religions, beginning with Buddhism.

Vision of Tarot is in this sense modeled on Langland's epic, *Piers Plowman*, and becomes a search for Truth. Buddhism, for example, is shown to be sufficient to withstand temptations, while Christianity is revealed as a manifestation of apostasy, a perverting and distorting of the original teachings of Christ, himself an impotent super-Kirlian healer. Then Brother Paul and Lee, the Mormon, digress from historical Christianity to review Mormonism, by way of a spirit-flight to the American continent (to the land of Lamanites, Nephites, and the *Book of Mormon*). Anthony uses the episode to condemn "schismatic Christianity," with its divergence from Christ's teaching and simultaneous (and paradoxical) dependence upon a man both mortal and human.

Again, Brother Paul emerges from the animation dissatisfied. In a final decision, he proposes to seek the truth about God by defining the inversion—Satan. Accompanied by the same group—each substantially and critically altered by the experiences of the previous animation—Paul descends into Hell in *Faith of Tarot*. In epical terminology, he journeys to the underworld for enlightenment and receives it. Confronted by Satan, Paul is able to extricate himself from satanic temptations sufficiently to earn three wishes—themselves forms of temptation. He uses the first to trace the true history of Tarot, the second to follow it into the future, and third (selfishly, he thinks) to save the life of a Solarian of the far future. For his selfishness, he resigns himself to Hell.

However, in giving up all for another sentient, he has in fact succeeded in avoiding the final strategem of Hell. He leaves, bringing with him essential information. He sees the future, including the vast empire supported by the triple principles of Aura, Tarot, and Animation. And like Neq before him, his self-sacrifice salvages some hope for the future.

In plot outline, the novels do not differ markedly from other Anthony works; in impact, however, they are far less effective. Anthony concentrates on horror and disgust until it begins to seem gratuitous. In a short story like "On the Uses of Torture," such elements are intrinsic to the plot. Without them, there would simply *be* no story. It is more difficult, however, to carry such involvement out over the space of a trilogy. Anthony does, of course, have some justification for the inclusion of these elements. He is, after all, discussing Hell, certainly not a nice place. And he is consistent in his portrayal of human nature, particularly when uncontrolled and allowed to follow its baser instincts. However, the frequent incidents of mutilation, castration, and overt perversion seem unconvincing in the long run. And for that reason, they irritate and offend rather than support Anthony's larger purposes.

The Planet of Tarot trilogy is certainly not for the squeamish, nor is it altogether for those who enjoyed the first installment of Tarot civilization in the Cluster novels. Anthony himself admits this. [12] While they do have merit and share some of his typical strengths of invention and energy, the novels of the trilogy remain less satisfying than most of his other works. They certainly pale beside the final completed series Anthony has written (to date), the Xanth novels.

NOTES:

1. *New York Times Book Review*, 25 December 1977, p. 11.
2. Anthony defines the Kirlian aura in this way: "Two and a half of their [Solarians'] millenia ago—that would be about thirty-five Quadpointers—before they strayed from their small dense homeplanet, there was a man named Kilner of London. He was a special kind of healer called a 'doctor' who worked with primitive radiation called 'X rays.' He became interested in stories of a numbus or invisible aura around living creatures that he thought reflected their states of health . . . . Thirty years after Kilner's observations, another man named Kirlian of Krasnodar managed to photograph the aura, that is, to make a sort of two-dimensional holograph of it, very crude. *Then* the Solarians began to believe" (*KQ*), Ch. 2).
3. Searles, p. 10.
4. Although *Thousandstar* and *Viscous Circle* take place in the same

society as the other novels, they are not a part of the action incorporated in the trilogy, but are instead branch adventures, fascinating in their own right, but unrelated to the larger scope of the trilogy.

5.   It should be noted that Anthony's interest in auras extends beyond merely using them as a structuring device in these novels. The word *aura* occurs, usually in critical passages, in nearly every novel and short story he has written.

6.   Biggers, p. 61.

7.   The derivation of the Cluster Tarot is explained in the subsequent Planet of Tarot series.

8.   "The Tarot in Charles Williams and Piers Anthony," presented to the Swann Conference, Florida Atlantic University, March 1981, pp. 5, 6.

9.   Biggers, p. 61.

10.   Biggers, p. 61.

11.   Biggers, p. 61.

12.   Biggers, p. 61.

VIII

XANTH

A Spell for Chameleon, *The Source of Magic*, *Castle Roogna*, and *Centaur Aisle*

The Xanth novels differ markedly from Anthony's other novels in some respects; yet in others, they neatly follow his progression of thought, theme and purpose. The series is unusual in that it has been classified as "juvenile fiction," although the novels are entirely enjoyable to adult readers. As Paul McGuire has argued,

> There are two points pertinent to classifying this novel [*SC*]. The first is that it is a juvenile or perhaps it would be more accurate to say a "for young adults."
>
> The second point, of course, is that the first point is meaningless. A rose is a rose and a good book is a good read. What's better, a very good juvenile or a mediocre adult novel? Between an excellent juvenile and an excellent adult novel which is greater, similarities or differences? Who loves a good juvenile novel more than an adult? [1]

The heroes of the three novels tend to be youngish; Bink is just short of twenty-five at the beginning of *A Spell for Chameleon* but seems much younger emotionally and psychologically—which is appropriate since the novel is an account of his maturing. In *The Source of Magic*, he is not much older chronologically. Dor, in *Castle Roogna*, is Bink's twelve-year old son, obsessed with breasts and bottoms as he discovers sexuality. And in *Centaur Aisle*, he is only sixteen—and a rather young and inexperienced sixteen, at that. So in that sense the books are definitely oriented toward younger readers.

They do, however, exert a strong appeal for readers of all ages, primarily because they are simply fun. In speaking of "On the Uses of Torture," Anthony commented that

> I wrote it a decade ago but could not get it published I

71

suspect it is the most brutal SF done. I like to do a good job of whatever I do—but mostly my taste runs to the more imaginative, lighter entertainment, these days. Reflects my increasing satisfaction with my life; it is hard to write brutal fiction when you have no basic frustrations greater than how a photograph looks. I've been trying to write horror fiction, and come up against that barrier: my heart just isn't in it. I no longer have a sufficiently twisted mind. Sigh. [2]

No reader of the Tarot series could accuse Anthony of either unbroken lightmindedness or of an aversion to horror. But in fact, Anthony's assessment of the state of his mind seems accurate. Against the God of Tarot series is set the adventures of Cluster trilogy, serious in their own way but infused with a spirit of inventiveness; or the fantasy worlds of Xanth, paradigms of ingenious fun; or the science-fiction/fantasy amalgam of *Split Infinity*, *Blue Adept*, and *Juxtaposition*. In these novels, Anthony releases his penchant for lightness and humor to an extent rarely seen in the earlier novels and in only a few of his short stories. But this sense of fun creates its own difficulties; like McGuire, I must hasten to add that the Xanth novels are "excellent and nowhere as silly as this review"—or this introduction. [3]

A Spell for Chameleon, nominee for the Hugo Award in 1978 as best book-length fantasy and winner of the August Derleth Fantasy Award, is a quest. In a land in which everyone has a magical talent, Bink apparently has none. He is supremely normal and, because of that, will be exiled from the magical land on his twenty-fifth birthday unless he can discover and prove his talent. He is accompanied on his quest by a variety of creatures, including a centaur and a griffin. He encounters an evil magician, exiled to Mundania (Xanth's magic-less neighbor) for his wickedness; a beautiful queen of illusion; and several girls who bear a striking resemblance to each other, primarily because they are merely different phases of the same woman, Chameleon. It ends happily, as a good fantasy must, with the hero discovering his talent and winning the girl.

The Source of Magic continues Bink's adventures. He is now happily married, but is nevertheless sent on a second quest—to discover the source of all magic in Xanth. The reader is again immersed in a whirlpool of fantasy, from which it seems at times that he will never quite emerge.

In *Castle Roogna*, Dor enters a magic tapestry and travels eight-hundred years into the past to discover a potion to revive Jonathan the Zombie, beloved of his nurse, Millie the ghost. He enters the Xanth of the past, a twelve-year old mind in the body of a mature male, accompanied by a giant spider. They in turn meet with nearly innumerable variations on fantasy characters.

Centaur Aisle, the first volume in a second trilogy (followed by *Ogre, Ogre* and *Night Mare*), is similarly a quest. King Trent and Queen Iris leave Xanth for what they intend as a short stay in Mundania. During their absence, Dor temporarily fills in as King—training for the time when he, as full Magician, will in fact become king. It soon becomes apparent, however, that Trent and Iris are not going to return as scheduled, and Dor sets out on a series of escapades that lead him through the entire length of Xanth (which is, as Anthony's map clearly shows, shaped suspiciously like Florida) and ultimately into Mundania. As he makes decisions and leads his band of fellow-adventurers deeper into Mundania, Dor undergoes an education that includes his first experiences with the possibility of mature sexuality.

In the series, Anthony balances between his own inherent energy and the requirements of plotting and narration—and occasionally overbalances. Algis Budrys pointed out a potential flaw in *The Source of Magic*, one which occasionally threatens the entire series:

> Anthony is one of those idiosyncratic persons who succeeds as a writer while violating many accepted rules on how prose is to be handled and storytelling is to be done . . . . Fast-paced adventure—in a story line that never sits still—carries the reader over the considerable barrier of Anthony's hectic style into an asset by sheer force of energy. [4]

A similar evaluation emphasizes Anthony's tight-rope walking between enough and too much:

> This is a readable, occasionally gripping fantasy about Bink, a hero too noble and pure to be likeable . . . . The characters and the prose have a penchant for cuteness; this is the central problem of the book. Nevertheless, the novel is redeemed by its inventiveness and charm. [5]

The series deals with maturity and control, but on a much narrower scale than Anthony has been used to. He is here concerned explicitly with a single individual—unusual only in possessing magical powers—rather than with the growth of a species, or planets, or stellar systems, or galaxies. The world of Xanth is narrower, but no less critical. Nor is it deficient in imagination. Anthony appears to have enjoyed his forays into Xanth, so much so that some readers have found its lushness of detail digressive:

> Piers Anthony, in his trilogy beginning with *A Spell for Chameleon*, apparently decided to invest his magical land of Xanth with every fantastical conception ever invented. It has quests, enchanted castles, riddles, unicorns, griffins, mermaids, giants (not to mention invisible giants), zombies, ghosts, elves, magicians, man-eating trees, enchantresses, and a host of inventions from Anthony's own fertile mind.

Every person, animal creature, plant, and even rock in Xanth is magic or has magical talent; the resulting stories are giddy, fast-paced as a Concorde, and a bit too cute for my taste. It's like Oz raised to the Nth power of bedlam.

On the plus side, the action is non-stop and the sheer amount of invention is awesome. On the negative side, there is the aforementioned cuteness which extends itself to a rather sniggery attitude toward sex and females that may set some people's teeth on edge. On my part, I'm not unhappy to see lovely Xanth sink slowly in the west. [6]

Yet there is more in the series than Baird Searles allows. Many of the elements mentioned are essentially Anthony: the concern for developing sexual awareness, most obvious in *Castle Roogna*, and *Centaur Aisle*, is occasionally irritating, yet at the same time is an outgrowth of the same sense of sexuality and identity that informs the serious novels, from *Chthon* and *Sos* through the Tarot series. The inventiveness has its analog in the multiple forms of sentient life inhabiting Anthony's worlds and serves the same function here: to suggest the interrelatedness of life, no matter how distant in form from human standards. The opening paragraph of *Spell* defines Anthony's concern for penetrating appearances to approach the essence:

A small lizard perched on a brown stone. Feeling threatened by the approach of human beings along the path, it metamorphosed into a stingray beetle, then into a stenchpuffer, then into a fiery salamander.

Bink smiled. These conversions weren't real. It had assumed the forms of obnoxious little monsters, but not their essence. It could not sting, stink, or burn. It was a chameleon, using its magic to mimic creatures of genuine threat (*SC*, Ch. 1).

In much the same way, Bink and Dor may have the forms of obnoxious heroes ("Dor is as insufferably noble as was his father, Bink...." [7], but in *essence*, they are part of a larger community of life.

Even the puns mentioned by nearly every reviewer are critically important to the novels. The readers who respond negatively to the punning are perhaps justified, since there are frequently long passages of narration whose sole function seems to be merely the setting up of a pun. Early in *Spell*, Bink remembers a lesson he had learned from his father some years earlier:

He remembered the wild oats he had planted as an adolescent. Sea oats were restless, but their cousins, the wild oats, were hyperactive. They had fought him savagely, their stems slashing across his wrists as he tried to harvest a ripe ear. He had gotten it, but had been uncomfortably scratched and abraded before getting clear of the patch. He had plant ed those few wild seeds in a secret plot behind his house, and watered them every day, the natural way. He had guarded the bad-tempered shoots from all harm, his antici pation growing. What an adventure for a teenaged male! Until his mother, Bianca, had discovered the plot. Alas, she had recognized the species immediately.

There had been a prompt family hassle. "How could you?" Bianca demanded, her face flaring. But Roland had labored to suppress his admiring smile. "Sowing wild oats!" he murmured. "The lad's growing up" (*SC*, Ch. 1).

Superficially, this seems precisely the sort of verbal excess that Paul McGuire and others found fault with—the whole digression apparently for the purpose of a pun. But the technique goes beyond merely the level of verbal humor—because in Xanth, "sowing wild oats" is not a metaphor. A serious reality underlies the expression:

Roland turned to Bink, shaking his head in a gesture that was only nominally negative. Roland was a powerful, hand some man and he had a special way with gestures. "Genuine wild oats, hulled thrashing from the stem, sown by the full moon, watered with your own urine?' he inquired frankly, and Bink nodded, his face at half heat. 'So that when the plants mature, and the oat nymph manifests, she will be bound to you, the fertilizer figure?" (*SC*, Ch. 1).

This level is more typically Anthony. Underlying the overt pun is a second—the "fertilizer" figure instead of the "fertility" figure—and all encompassing a sweeping inversion of the reader's objective reality. Such events would be mythical in Mundania, but Anthony's story takes place in Xanth, which is itself an inversion of scientific realities. There magic is natural: sowing wild oats is no metaphor, but a statement of fact and intention. From that reality, Roland provides Bink with a lesson in maturity:

Roland's face became serious. "To a young man, inex perienced, the notion of a lovely, nude, captive nymph can be phenomenally tempting," he continued. "All the physical attributes of a real woman, and none of the mental ones. But, son, this is a juvenile dream, like finding a candy tree. The reality would not be all you anticipated. One quickly becomes surfeited, tired of unlimited candy, and so it also is with—with a mindless female body. A man cannot love a nymph. She might as well be air. His ardor rapidly turns to boredom, and to disgust . . . . Son, what you need is a real, live girl.

A figure with personality, who will talk back to you. It is far more challenging to develop a relationship with a complete woman, and often extremely frustrating . . . . But in the long run it is also far more rewarding. What you sought in the wild oats was a shortcut—but in life there are no shortcuts" (*SC*, Ch. 1).

The pun ultimately augments Anthony's purposes in the novel—to detail the process of Bink's growth.

Because Xanth is a magical land, Anthony frequently uses inversions of norms. Magic in Xanth is natural, normal, useful; anything mundane—i.e., produced by science or explained by science—is unnatural and suspect, not to be believed:

> Bink and Chester dismounted and walked beside the worm, here on the street. Soon a magic wagon rolled up. It resembled a monster-drawn coach, but lacked the monster. The wheels were fat bouncy donuts of rubber, and the body seemed to be metal. A purring emanated from the interior. There was probably a little monster inside, pedaling the wheels (*SM*, Ch. 10).

A monster-drawn coach fits neatly into the norms of Xanth. Consequently, the internal combustion engine—the automobile—must be defined in terms of the magical to be comprehended.

On a somewhat more sophisticated level, language becomes a powerful tool in creating Anthony's fantasy universe. From his earliest story, "Possible to Rue," Anthony has shown an abiding interest in the potentials of language, including metaphors and puns. In Xanth, he incorporates much of this interest in language in furthering the plot and in establishing the essence of his fantasy universe. In Xanth, language is literal, especially what in Mundania would be called metaphors. Thus breadfruit trees bear loaves of bread; shoetrees bear shoes in varying sizes and styles; nickelpedes are like centipedes, only five times larger and more vicious; and sunflowers are flowers whose blossoms are tiny suns blazing at the top of the stalk—a potent weapon if an enemy looks directly at them. [8]

This is the magic of Xanth; Anthony enables the reader to look at the old and stale with new eyes, to see realities hidden behind the figurative language of Mundania. For a moment, the reader begins to believe in the words he hears daily and, then suddenly, realizes that he is being forced to listen carefully to those words. With that comes the awareness that the things for which those words stand in Xanth are not at all what one might expect. And just as suddenly, Xanth comes to life, surrounded by magic; Mundania seems a distant, drab, and distorted memory in contrast.

The Xanth novels are difficult to classify, difficult to summarize.

To list in order the various episodes Bink survives would be pointless—and would, as McGuire suggested, make the whole series seem silly. Yet to read them is to invite entertainment on the highest level. To cite William Glass' analysis of *Castle Roogna*:

> Piers Anthony's *A Spell for Chameleon* and *The Source of Magic*, his first two novels about the magical land of Xanth, were the most entertaining and fun novels he's done in years. Now we have *Castle Roogna*. And this third Xanth novel is even more fun than its predecessors . . . .
>
> Anthony is clearly having fun. His wordplay shades from the cockeared literal (shoes plucked from shoe-trees, milk gotten from milkweeds) through the offhandedly excruciating (the castle ghosts are shy and "easily spooked") to the openly satirical (as in Dor's rather harrowing battle with the uncontainable Gerrymander).
>
> This is whimsical, rigorously consistent fantasy, like that encouraged by John W. Campbell in the early 1940's . . . .
>
> At the same time, *Castle Roogna* is also constantly (if entertainingly) didactic, in something like Heinlein's SF juveniles of the 1950's. Dor is clearly the naive Heinlein youth, his quest their usual one for competence and maturity—even if it is complicated by tritons, dragons, ogres, zombies, tangle trees, forfons, and the like; and even if the older, Heinlein competent man character is a very intelligent, highly magnified spider. [9]

This is not to suggest that the novels are perfect. There are difficulties, both conceptual and stylistic. The episodic nature of *Source of Magic* becomes a bit wearing. The final chapters of that novel attempt to establish something of the seriousness of earlier works—not entirely successfully in the case of Anthony's complex description of the demon Zanth, his purposes, and his meaning. [10] And more critically, there is rarely any sense of actual threat in the series. Bink, Dor, and the others encounter magical, dangerous beasts and make their ways through perilous territory, but only occasionally does Anthony convince the reader that the apparent dangers are more than superficial. Magic comes too easily—especially in *Centaur Aisle*, where Anthony becomes more overt in supplying solutions to problems just before the problem arises, as in the rainbow sequence of Chapter 8. But in general the series is that rather rare phenomenon—a performance that surmounts its flaws.

Piers Anthony is an author with a special following, as befits someone whose style is markedly individual. Wordy, fond of unpronounceable or ineuphorious invented terms, repetitious, in many ways infuriating to writers of the tale plainly told, he nevertheless triumphs over what would be short-comings in someone more self-conscious about these matters. [11]

What Budrys said here about *Castle Roogna* is applicable to virtually all of Anthony's fiction. In each story or novel, there seems to be some impediment to clear, easy reading: the ritualizing in *Battle Circle*, the erratic, mythopoeic time-warping in *Chthon* and *Pthor*; digressions into paleontology, geology and history in the Omnivore trilogy; the astrological analogies in *Macroscope*; the Tarot and Kirlian auras, coupled with typographical experimentation in the Cluster trilogy; the invidious weaving of dream and reality in the Tarot trilogy and its descent into horror and disgust; and the language and too-lush invention of Xanth. Yet in spite of these difficulties, each novel, each set of novels, justifies itself and its author on its own grounds: as entertainment, as literature, and as thoughtful explorations into a multitude of ideas essential to humanity, civilization, and life.

NOTES:

1. "Review: *A Spell for Chameleon*," *Science Fiction Review*, February 1978, p. 45.
2. Letter to Michael Collings, 7 June 1980.
3. McGuire, p. 45.
4. *Booklist*, 1 September 1979, p. 29.
5. *Publishers Weekly*, 14 May 1979, p. 209.
6. "On Books," *Isaac Asimov's Science Fiction Magazine*, September 1979, p. 18.
7. *Publishers Weekly*, 14 May 1979, p. 209.
8. For a fuller discussion of this technique, see Michael R. Collings, "Words and Worlds: The Creation of the Fantasy Universe in Zelazny, Lee, and Anthony," presented to the Swann Conference, Florida Atlantic University, March 1980.
9. *Science Fiction Review*, November 1979, pp. 47-48.
10. Collings, pp. 20-21.
11. Budrys, p. 24.

IX

SHORT FICTION

Anthony's literary reputation rests primarily on his novels, for several good reasons. With the exception of "On the Uses of Torture," published in 1981 but written some years earlier, only a few stories have appeared since 1972, during which time he has published over twenty-five novels. Many of the earlier stories have been incorporated into subsequent novels: The Doctor Dillingham series appeared in 1971 as *Prosth Plus*, the intergalactic adventures of a dentist. [1] Similarly, "The Alien Rulers" (1968) provided the basis for the expanded *Triple Detente* (1974). Anthony has published only about thirty stories (a ratio of only one story published for each four written), far fewer than his total number of novels. [2]

The paucity of stories is not a substantial problem, however, since Anthony's energy, so essential to his success, demands a larger stage, both physically and creatively, through the enhanced opportunities for invention that the novel requires. His short stories, while interesting, tend to be rather thin, depending upon a single effect supported by an exotic imagination, as in "Wood You?" (1970), with the pun implicit in the title. An additional difficulty is that his stories are difficult to locate. Only two are currently in print: "In the Barn," in *Again, Dangerous Visions* and "On the Uses of Torture," in *The Berkeley Showcase* (Vol. 3). Most of the remaining stories appeared in science-fiction magazines, many no longer readily accessible. [3]

Several stories, however, merit attention. In 1963, Anthony published his first two stories: "Possible to Rue" and "Quinquepedalian." They are interesting in terms of Anthony's development as a writer since they display two elements that have continued unabated in his prose. The first, most apparent in "Possible to Rue," is his love of word games. Although the story focuses on a perennial Anthony topic—the relationship between man and other forms of life, here treated as if man had voluntarily relinquished his part of the relationship—the story is structured around a pun. As the characters check encyclopedia entries and discover that all animals—both legendary and real, including horses and rocs—are listed as mythical, they discover that it is "possible to rue" the disappearance of animals from the world. And when the boy finally asks about the roc, his father reaches for the appropriate volume, with "Possible to Rue" imprinted on the spine.

In the second story, "Quinquepedalian," Anthony shows the richness of invention that would characterize all of his later fictions. The title refers to a five-legged monster, so huge that human explorers at first mistake it for a tree. It attacks when a member of the party kills a smaller, twenty-foot Quink. The remainder of the story recounts the humans' attempts to escape the parent Quink, and Tinnerman's gradual unraveling of the secrets of the alien life form, including the startling discovery that it is an amalgam of seven separate brains. He responds to the monster in a way that is typical of most of Anthony's heroes:

> "Quinquepedalian, septecerebrian—you are probably smarter than I." And certainly stronger. He thought about that, discovering a weird pleasure in the contemplation of it. All his life he had remained aloof from his fellows, searching for something he could honestly look up to. Now he had found it (p. 130).

The conclusion of the story illustrates an early version of another consistent element in Anthony, the need for understanding and compromise among sapient species:

> Quink was stalking him with ageless determination and rapidly increasing sagacity. Already she had learned to anticipate the geometric patterns he traced. He had led her through a simple square, triangle and star, giving up each figure when she solved it and sent her body to intercept him ahead. Soon she would come to the conclusion that the prey was something more than a vicious rodent. Once she realized that she was dealing with intelligence, communication would begin (p. 130).

The attitude toward human beings, toward aliens (and meticulously constructed aliens at that), and toward inter-species communication and relationships inherent in "Quinquepedalian" are hallmarks of Anthony's prose over the nearly twenty years separating the story from his most recent work, *Mutes*.

In 1965, he published "Phog," a story concerning an unseen creature living in a fog. It was well received by other science-fiction writers and particularly fascinated Roger Zelazny. Anthony apparently enjoyed the story as well; he refers to it in *OX*, published eleven years later. In the next year, an unusual triple collaboration with Robert E. Margroff and Andrew J. Moffutt resulted in "Mandroid," an investigation into man's relationships with other sentients, in this case humanoid androids. The same year, he received a Nebula nomination for another collaboration, "The Message," written with Frances Hall.

He subsequently received awards nominations for "Getting Through University" (Hugo, 1969), one of the Dr. Dillingham series; "The Bridge" (Nebula, 1970); and "In the Barn" (Nebula, 1972). "The Bridge" emphasizes Anthony's interest in blending sexuality and science ficton. At the same time, it illustrates his consistent awareness of energy as vital to supporting civilization, a theme developed in *Macroscope*, published a year earlier. In "The Bridge," there is an interstellar transfer of energy, much like that contemplated by the Andromedans in the Cluster novels, except that in this case, the Oomians successfully transfer human semen through the agency of a six-inch female. The story is startling in its sexuality, but well constructed, with a number of literary and mythic patterns interwoven throughout, including that of the rise and fall of Troy (both the Homeric city and the hero, Troy Burg; again the name is a double pun). "The Bridge" attempts to define the essential nature of sexuality, using it as a metaphor for relationships. The consummation of the sex act restores vigor to an energy-depleted race and simultaneously provides Burg with someone he is capable of loving fully.

Anthony's most important story is "In the Barn." In the headnote to the story, Harlan Ellison says that "More than any other writer, Piers Anthony is responsible for there *being* an *Again, Dangerous Visions....*" [4] The story exemplifies the sort of fiction Ellison had included in *Dangerous Visions*. Hitch, the main character, investigates alternate-Earth #772, a world with no mammals other than humans, but where livestock is paradoxically the main business:

> Barns were everywhere, and milk was a staple industry—yet there were no cows or goats or similar domesticants (p. 393).

With Swiftian bitterness, Anthony reveals that humans provide the breeding stock. Hitch becomes increasingly involved with the alternate-Earth, transferring his emotional conflicts over an earthside romance to one of the "females" in the barn. The story is graphic, both in sexuality and in brutality, a convincing statement of Anthony's belief in the rights of all life forms.

The story evoked immediate controversy, as Anthony apparently intended. In speaking of the genesis of the story, and of reactions to it, he recently wrote:

> I did that story to prove that I could make the standard Ellison set in *Dangerous Visions* . . . but two reviews of the story were highly negative. No, not reviews by people afraid of sex . . . . They said I had poor characterization. I don't really argue with that; characterization was not what I was trying for in that story. A third comment . . . dismissed it as "vegetarian SF." I am a vegetarian, but this was not that kind of fiction

either. If I ever do the sequel story, *that* will be vegetarian, about the slaughterhouse on that planet-frame: identical to those of this world, with the same substitution of one mammal for another. [5]

There is more to the story than characterization or vegetarianism—or explicit sex, for that matter. It is Anthony at his most powerful, drawing uncomfortably close parallels between the worlds of his imagination and the reader's world. The force of "In the Barn" stems primarily from the detail Anthony infuses into an otherwise straightforward, purposefully shocking plot; the detail creates a sense of verisimilitude that is suddenly inverted when the essential difference between Earth Prime and #772 is defined.

A similar technique operates in the roughly contemporary piece, "On the Uses of Torture." The story was unsalable at the time it was written. Only after nearly a decade has it been published and then with the editorial comment that it is "one of the most revolting we've read. It is exploitative, bludgeoning, and completely, utterly compelling." [6] The warning is wholly justified; Anthony has claimed that it is perhaps "the most brutal SF ever done." [7] The claim is most probably true.

Unlike many of Anthony's characters, the narrator of "On the Uses of Torture" is not admirable. He is in charge of discipline in a prison camp and conversant with the uses of torture—the normal, conventional uses, that is, subjecting his men to a painbox that stimulates nerves without damaging tissue. He is ruthless, as he must be to survive, carefully assessing both his ambitions, potential, and the men he must control. Anthony does not whitewash the unsavory character: he is a monster of callousness, insensitivity, and exploitative ambition. But he has one redeeming feature—he subjects himself to the same standards that he demands of others.

To rise in the hierarchy of his society, he volunteers for an extraordinarily difficult mission. Six envoys have been sent to the critical planet of Waterloo to negotiate for trading rights. Five never returned, and the sixth escaped with a mutilated hand and stories of torture. If the hero (unnamed, since the story is in the first person) succeeds, he will be in a position to enforce a treaty with the natives.

What happens is gruesome in the extreme—the systematic dismemberment of his body, told in first-person, present tense. It is the epitome of brutality and horror; yet like its essentially reprehensible character, the story has redeeming qualities. Through it, Anthony literally strips his Everyman-character of pretensions, using the most effective tool possible—pain and torture. At the end, the narrator thinks:

My legs are gone, my right arm, my remaining ear and nostril. I am blind. No teeth remain in my jaws. The waste products of my body drip down from a gash like that of a woman. But I can hear, for they dare not touch my inner ear lest they damage the brain and bring death (pp. 98-99).

In this condition, he is told that he has attained a degree of honor and authority attained by

Perhaps only two or three in each category, each year. Since your category is political, you are now qualified to join the governing council of Waterloo—the only alien ever to achieve this distinction. You have proven yourself by your steadfastness, and you have divested yourself of material considerations that might have biased a lesser individual. Thus you now have the potential for true objectivity, and can be a fitting ruler. Are you willing to accept this position? (p. 99).

His response establishes his understanding of the "uses of torture":

The torture gauntlet is a ladder to prominence, not with respect to competitors but to the society itself. The more the subject can take, the greater his reward. And Kule is correct: of course I can no longer be bribed by any of the physical pleasures. I have no nose for perfume, no taste buds for food, no eyes for beauty, no phallus for sex. Money. What could it buy for me?
    I am indeed objective (p. 99).

Horrible as it is, the story investigates an alternative to self-serving, corrupt governments (about which Anthony has few delusions).
    Unfortunately, there is one problem with the solution. By the end of the story, the narrator has expressed doubts about his sanity—and the reader quickly agrees. The final lines—

I have heard it said that power tends to corrupt. I wonder whether misery tends to ennoble?
    Yes—yes it does! I can offer no finer example of that than myself (p. 101)—

are more frightening than the tortures described. They come immediately after the narrator has decided to torture his fiance, who has followed him to the planet out of her love for him. He has been stripped of subjectivity, of preconceptions, of biases—and also of his humanity and his sanity. He has earned a place for himself in the highest councils of society. He is now as alien to the reader as was his erstwhile torturer/ interrogator, referring to "We Loos" and concluding that "Our program is unimaginative." He turns his mind to devising even more ingenious, rigorous methods of torture.

P. Schuyler Miller has referred to "In the Barn" as Swiftian, a satire on human Yahoos. [8] The same can be said about "On the Uses of Torture." The narrator, like Gulliver in Book Four, of *Gulliver's Travels*, becomes convinced of his species' inferiority before the alien race. In the end, he identifies completely with them, struggling to think like them, to become like them. And like Gulliver, the narrator of "On the Uses of Torture" becomes quite, quite mad.

It would be tempting to mention other stories but enough has been said here to suggest that they, like Anthony's novels, are intriguing combinations of daring conceptual development, intriguing imaginative effects, and overriding concern for humanity. Piers Anthony may not be one of the giants of science fiction; he is, however, a solidly respectable figure, one who repays his readers with novels and stories that stimulate, entertain, and demand.

NOTES:

1. *A Readers Guide to Science Fiction* says about the series,

> *Prostho Plus* is a novel that in other hands might have been just plain silly, but Anthony makes this farce about the kidnapping and education of one Dr. Dillingham, a forty-three year old dentist from Earth, by an exotic array of aliens, a living satire of space opera, soap opera, and pretensions (p. 9).

2. Biggers, p. 58.
3. Unfortunately, many of Anthony's novels are also out of print and available only through outlets for used books. Among these are *ESP Worm*, *Race Against Time*, the Jason Striker novels, *The Ring*, and *Rings of Ice*.
4. *Again, Dangerous Visions*, p. 385.
5. Letter, 7 June 1980.
6. *Berkley Showcase*, III, 79.
7. Letter, 7 June 1980.
8. "The Reference Library," *Analog*, April 1973, p. 169.

X

SELECTIVELY ANNOTATED PRIMARY BIBLIOGRAPHY

1. NOVELS

Amazon Slaughter. New York: Berkley, 1976 [with Roberto Fuentes]. The fifth volume in the Jason Striker Series. Striker confronts Fu Antos (Fuentes and Anthony), Lord of the Ninja, in the wilderness of the Amazon Basin. The Striker novels are included here, both because they continue Anthony's interests in a number of themes (including the uses of torture and control) and because they have strong science-fictional elements.

The Bamboo Bloodbath. New York: Berkley, 1974 [with Roberto Fuentes]. The third of the Striker novels. Striker faces hyenas—both literal and figurative—in this tale of blackmail and martial arts, set largely in Florida.

Battle Circle. New York: Avon, 1978. The omnibus re-issuing of *Sos the Rope, Var the Stick*, and *Neq the Sword* (see below).

Blue Adept. New York: Ballantine, 1981. The second volume in the Proton/Phaze series. Stile, in his capacity as Blue Adept, one of the master magicians of Phaze, must track down his enemy, the Red Adept, both in the fantasy world of Phaze and the science-fictional world of Proton.

But What of Earth? Toronto, Canada: Laser Books, 1976 [Disputed collaboration with Robert Coulson]. When mattermission becomes a reality, Scot applies for a permit to emigrate to a colony planet. Refused permission, he must come to grips with an Earth in which normal societal patterns have been destroyed, and decreasing energy has reduced life to a barbaric, tribal form. Brother Paul of the Holy Order of Vision (Cluster and Tarot series) plays a major role.

Castle Roogna. New York: Ballantine, 1979. Volume three of the Xanth trilogy. Bink's son Dor passes through a magical tapestry and into the body of a Xanth soldier living eight-hundred years in the past. His only companion is a giant sentient spider.

Centaur Aisle. New York: Ballantine, 1982. The fourth Xanth novel and the beginning of a second trilogy. Dor, now sixteen, becomes temporary King of Xanth and must handle not only domestic problems, but also the quest for the missing King Trent and Queen Iris. His travels take him the length of Xanth and beyond, into Mundania.

Chaining the Lady. New York: Avon, 1978. Volume two of the Cluster trilogy. Melody of Mintake must marshal the forces of the Milky Way to battle the Andromedan threat of Kirlian hostaging.

Chthon. New York: Ballantine, 1967. Anthony's first published novel, receiving both Nebula and Hugo nominations. Aton Five, imprisoned in the caverns of Chthon, must escape both his physical and emotional prison, and solve the conflict of the Minionette. Sequel: *Phthor* (see below).

Cluster. New York: Avon, 1977. Volume one of the Cluster trilogy. Flint of Outworld travels by means of Kirlian transfer to alien Spheres within the Milky Way, with the two-fold purpose of spreading the knowledge of Kirlian transfer among other sentients and of countering Andromedan incursions into his galaxy.

ESP Worm. New York: Paperback Library, 1970 [with Robert E. Margroff]. An intelligent, powerful telepathic worm disrupts Earth society. Because it is a juvenile, it has no inhibitions and creates tremendous confusion until finally returned to its parents.

Faith of Tarot. New York: Berkley, 1980. The third volume in the Planet of Tarot trilogy. Brother Paul and his companions undergo an aura-animation that entails a descent into Hell, leading to the unveiling of the true God of Planet Tarot.

God of Tarot. New York: Jove, 1979. Volume one of the Planet of Tarot trilogy. Brother Paul of the Holy Order of Vision is assigned to visit Planet Tarot and determine which of the various manifestations of God that have appeared there is true.

Hasan. San Bernardino, CA: Borgo Press, 1977. An Arabian romance, in which Hasan, poor son of a merchant, is lured by an alchemist into the legendary land of Serendip, where he falls in love with the elusive Bird Princess.

Juxtapositon. New York: Ballantine, 1982. The conclusion to the Proton/Phaze trilogy. Stile becomes more deeply enmeshed in power struggles among the Citizens of Proton and the Adepts of Phaze and in his own emotional involvement with the robot Sheen and Lady Blue. Stile must somehow determine how to resolve his own problems, while simultaneously uncovering a plot that threatens the existence of both frames.

Kiai! New York: Berkley, 1974 [with Roberto Fuentes]. The first of the Jason Striker novels. In a setting reminiscent of the Battle Circle of *Sos, Var,* and *Neq,* Striker meets the top representatives of each martial art.

Kirlian Quest. New York: Avon, 1978. The third volume of the Cluster trilogy. Herald the Healer wins and loses the beautiful Psyche of Kade, then must set out on an odyssey to save the galaxy from the Space Amoeba and unravel the final riddles of the Ancients.

Macroscope. New York: Avon, 1969. Hugo nominee, 1970. Ivo Archer and four others attempt to circumvent the Destroyer beam intercepted by the macroscope. In doing so, they discover the Traveler beam and initiate an extra-galactic fight that ultimately helps humanity gain its rightful place in galactic civilization.

The Magic of Xanth. Garden City, NY: Nelson Doubleday [Science Fiction Book Club], [1981]. The Science Fiction Book Club omnibus edition of the Xanth trilogy, *A Spell for Chameleon*, *The Source of Magic*, and *Castle Roogna*.

Mistress of Death. New York: Berkley, 1974 [with Roberto Fuentes]. The second novel of the Jason Striker Series. Jason Striker meets his match in Ilunga, the Black Karate Mistress.

Mutes. New York: Avon, 1981. The mutant Knot confronts Finesse, an agent of the galactic Coordinating Computer and must decide whether to serve the Computer or oppose it. In his adventures, he must also weld a confederacy between humans and non-human sentients to preserve galactic civilization.

Neq the Sword. London: Corgi, 1975. The third of the Battle Circle series. After the brutal murder of his wife, Neq undertakes a series of wandering, punctuated by violent revenge on the circle society. Finally, he turns his efforts to re-building Helicon and restoring order to society.

Night Mare. New York: Ballantine, 1982. The sixth of the Xanth series.

Ninja's Revenge. New York: Berkley, 1975 [with Roberto Fuentes]. The fourth novel in the Jason Striker Series. Striker must help build the Black Fortress of Fu Antos.

Ogre, Ogre. New York: Ballantine, 1983. The fifth of the Xanth series.

Omnivore. New York: Ballantine, 1968. The first of the Omnivore trilogy. Veg, Aquilon, and Cal must gradually reveal to the agent Subble their experiences on the fungoid planet Nacre, and the danger that threatens all life on Earth.

Orn. Garden City, NY: Nelson Doubleday [Science Fiction Book Club], 1971. The second of the Omnivore trilogy. The three explorers, with their mantas, are transported to Paleo, an alternate-Earth, where they encounter Orn, a sentient avian, and discover an enclave of dinosaurs. Together, they attempt to preserve Paleo from exploitation by Earth agents.

OX. Garden City, NY: Nelson Doubleday [Science Fiction Book Club], 1976. The third volume of the Omnivore trilogy. Humans, mantas, Orns, and agents undergo a series of adventures on multiple alternate frames, all part of the experiment designed by the sparkle-cloud entities to discover true sapience.

Phthor. New York: Berkley, 1975. Sequel to *Chthon*. Aton's son Arlo continues his struggles with the cavern-entity Chthon. His experiences lead inevitably to Ragnarok, the climactic battle between

Life and the mineral intellects.

Pretender. San Bernardino, CA: Borgo Press, 1979 [with Frances Hall]. Historical science-fiction novel set in ancient Babylon at the time of its fall to Cyrus. An alien intellect inhabits a boy's mind, guiding him through a number of adventures.

Prostho Plus. London: Victor Gollancz, 1971. The collected adventures of Dr. Dillingham, a dentist kidnapped by aliens. His patients include butterfly-people, whale-like sentients, and an assortment of other oddities.

Race Against Time. New York: Hawthorn Books, 1973. Six children discover that they are being kept in artificial enclaves and that they are the last representatives of distinct races remaining on a devastated Earth.

The Ring. New York: Ace, 1968 [with Robert E. Margroff]. Jeff Font, a condemned criminal, is "ringed," sentenced to wear a device guaranteed to make all citizens law-abiding. But Jeff is not willing to accept his sentence without fighting back.

Rings of Ice. New York: Avon, 1974. A small group of survivors try to maintain stability, order, and life itself on a world suddenly deluged by a series of month-long storms.

The Source of Magic. New York: Ballantine, 1979. The second volume of the Xanth series. Bink and his companions must seek out and identify the source of all magic in Xanth.

A Spell for Chameleon. New York: Ballantine, 1977. Hugo nominee, 1978. The first volume of the Xanth series. Bink is apparently magicless in a magical land. To avoid exile, he must go on a quest to define his magical talent.

Split Infinity. New York: Ballantine, 1980. Volume One of the Proton/Phaze trilogy. Stile, a jockey on Proton, discovers the existence of the fantasy alternate, Phaze. Someone has attempted to kill him on Proton; his alternate on Phaze, the Blue Adept, has already been murdered. Stile sets out to find out why.

Steppe. London: Millington, 1976. Alp, a ninth-century warrior from the Steppes of Russia, is suddenly transported into the twenty-fourth century to become a player in the Game, a computer-controlled reconstruction of history.

Thousandstar. New York: Avon, 1980. A companion to the Cluster series. Heem of Highfalls and Jessica of Capella, sharing a single body, compete with other sentient duos for control of an unexplored Ancient site.

Triple Detente. New York: DAW, 1974. An over-crowded, polluted, energy-depleted Earth is taken over by conquering Aliens—while the Earth forces take over the Alien homeworld. Each must establish order and control on their respective planets. Then a third sentient civilization is discovered, and the fragile balance is disrupted.

Var the Stick. London: Faber and Faber, 1972. The second novel in the Battle Circle trilogy. The mutant Var deserts the Battle Circle society and undertakes an odyssey through northern America and Canada and into China, accompanied only by a young girl. On the way, they see how other peoples have adapted to the ruin caused by the Blast.

Viscous Circle. New York: Avon, 1982. Solarians invade the Band System in search of a functional Ancient Site. Rondl, an amnesiac band who understands concepts alien to others of his species, must discover both who he is and how he can stop the Solarians from destroying Band society.

Vision of Tarot. New York: Berkley, 1980. Volume two in the Planet of Tarot series. Brother Paul and his companions use aura-animations and the Tarot to investigate the history of religions, as part of their quest for the identity of the God of planet Tarot.

2. SHORT STORIES

"The Alien Rulers," *Analog,* March 1968, 8-39.

"Beak by Beak," *Analog,* December 1967, pp. 97-105.

"Black Baby," *Worlds of If,* September-October 1972, pp. 64-82.

"The Bridge," *Worlds of Tomorrow,* 1970, pp. 75-85, 155-158. Nebula nomination, 1970.

"Encounter," *Fantastic,* October 1964, pp. 104-111.

"Equals Four," *Worlds of If,* July-August 1970, pp. 51-63, 155-157.

"Getting Through University," *Worlds of If,* August 1968, pp. 8-34.

"The Ghost Galaxies," *Worlds of If,* September 1966, pp. 96-116.

"Hard Sell," *Worlds of If,* August 1972, pp. 143-158.

"Hearts," *Books and Bookmen,* December 1970, p. 7.

"Hasan," *Fantastic,* December 1969, pp. 6-83; February 1970, pp. 32-108.

"Hurdle," *Worlds of If,* November-December 1972, pp. 118-145.

"In the Barn." In *Again, Dangerous Visions.* Ed. Harlan Ellison. Garden City, NY: Doubleday, 1972, pp. 392-419. Nebula nominee, 1972.

"In the Jaws of Danger," *Worlds of If,* November 1967, pp. 106-120.

"Ki," *Vertex,* June 1974, pp. 40-43, 49-51, 65 [with Roberto Fuentes].

"Kiai—How it Began," *Deadly Hands of Kung Fu,* June 1975, pp. 34-40.

"The Life of Stripe," *Fantastic,* February 1969, pp. 49-51.

"Mandroid," *Worlds of If,* June 1966, pp. 6-50 [with Robert E. Margroff and Andrew J. Offutt].

"The Message," *Analog,* July 1966, pp. 8-36 [with Frances Hall]. Nebula nominee, 1966.

"Monarch," *Worlds of If,* November 1970, pp. 124-148.

"None But I," *Worlds of If,* October 1969, pp. 28-52, 160.

"On the Uses of Torture." In *The Berkley Showcase.* Ed. Victoria Schochet and John Silbersack. Vol. III, New York: Berkley, 1981, pp. 79-101.

"Orn," *Amazing*, July 1970, pp. 6-65, 128-140; September 1970, pp. 28-107.

"Payoff," *Adam Bedside Reader*," June 1966, pp. 22-25, 40-41, 48-49. [with Robert E. Margroff; under the pseudonym of "Robert Piers"].

"Phog," *Fantastic*, June 1975, pp. 97-107.

"Possible to Rue," *Fantastic*, April 1963, pp. 120-123.

"Prostho Plus," *Analog*, November 1967, pp. 53-65.

"Quinquepedalian," *Amazing*, November 1963, pp. 106-121, 130.

"Scheol," *Analog*, September 1964, pp. 50-55 [with H. James Hotaling].

"Small Mouth, Bad Taste." In *Science Against Man*. Ed. Anthony Cheetham. New York: Avon, 1970, pp. 157-173.

"Sos the Rope," *Fantasy and Science Fiction*," July 1968, pp. 4-52; August 1968, pp. 26-50; September 1968, pp. 45-94.
   Hugo nominee, 1968; $5000 Science Fiction Novel Award

"Three Misses," *Deadly Hands of Kung Fu*, May 1976, pp. 28-36.

"Up Schist Creek." In *Generation*. Ed. David Gerrold. New York: Dell, 1972, pp. 20-40.

"The Whole Truth." In *Nova One: An Anthology of Original Science Fiction*. Ed. Harry Harrison. New York: Delacorte Press, 1970, pp. 209-222.

"Within the Cloud," *Galaxy*, April 1967, pp. 163-165.

"Wood You?" *Fantasy and Science Fiction*, October 1970, pp. 49-57.

3. NON-FICTION

"Alf Laylah Wa Laylah." *Niekas*, 1966.
   Discussion of Arabian mythic patterns.

"Index to Book Reviews." In *Index to the Science Fiction and Fantasy Magazines*. Comp. Al Lewis. Los Angeles, 1964.

Anthony contributed heavily to magazines, both articles and letters. Most of his early contributions are now difficult to trace down.

4. ANTHONY'S SERIES

Chthon Series:
   Chthon
   Phthor
Battle Circle Trilogy:
   Sos the Rope
   Var the Stick
   Neq the Sword
Omnivore Trilogy:
   Omnivore
   Orn
   OX

Cluster Series: [1]
   Cluster
   Chaining the Lady
   Kirlian Quest
   Thousandstar (while not a part of the Cluster Trilogy, this novel shares a common setting, time-frame, and characterization with the other three.)
   Viscous Circle
Magic of Xanth Trilogy:
   A Spell for Chameleon
   The Source of Magic
   Castle Roogna
   Centaur Aisle
   Ogre, Ogre
   Night Mare
Planet of Tarot Trilogy: [1]
   God of Tarot
   Faith of Tarot
   Vision of Tarot
Proton/Phaze Trilogy:
   Split Infinity
   Blue Adept
   Juxtaposition
Jason Striker Martial Arts Series (with Roberto Fuentes):
   Kiai!
   Mistress of Death
   Bamboo Bloodbath
   Ninja's Revenge
   Amazon Slaughter

1. *But What of Earth?* connects the two later trilogies through the introduction of Brother Paul of the Holy Order of Vision, but is not an integral part of either series.

SELECTIVELY ANNOTATED SECONDARY BIBLIOGRAPHY

Biggers, Cliff. "An Interview with Piers Anthony," *Science Fiction Review*, November 1977, pp. 56-62 [First published in *Future Retrospective*]. A largely autobiographical interview, with some insights into the relationship between Anthony's life and his writing. Includes discussions of works from *Chthon* through the Planet of Tarot series.

Brigg, Peter. "Analogies of Scale in Piers Anthony's *Macroscope*," *Science Fiction Studies*, 2 (1975), 119-130. Analyzes the methods by which Anthony presents relationships between macrocosm and microcosm in the novel; one of the few—and earliest—critical studies of Anthony.

Collings, Michael R. "Words and Worlds: The Creation of a Fantasy Universe in Zelazny, Lee, and Anthony." Unpublished paper presented to the Swann Conference on the Fantastic, Florida Atlantic University, March 1980. Compares the approaches to creating a fantastic/imaginary world in the three authors. The section on Anthony concentrates on language and linguistic inversion in the Xanth novels.

_____. "The Mechanisms of Fantasy," *The Lamp-Post of the Southern California C. S. Lewis Society*, 4, No. 3-4 (August-November 1980), 13-14, 16. A comparison of fantasy structures in several authors, including Zelazny, Anthony, and Lewis. The emphasis is on Lewis, and the ways his Space Trilogy is atypical of the SF norm, as exemplified by Anthony and the others.

Currey, L. W., ed. *Science Fiction and Fantasy Authors: A Bibliography of First Printings of their Fiction*. Boston, MA: G. K. Hall, 1979. A descriptive bibliography of Anthony's first editions.

Nasso, Christine, ed. *Contemporary Authors*. Rev. ed. Vol. 21-24. Detroit, Michigan: Gale Research Company, 1977. Biographical sketch of Anthony.

Pendexter, Hugh. "The Tarot in Charles Williams and Piers Anthony." Unpublished paper presented to the Swann Conference on the Fantastic, Florida Atlantic University, March 1981. A generalized treatment of the Tarot; comments at length on Anthony's modifications of the Tarot to suit his purposes in the Cluster novels.

Searles, Baird, et al. *Reader's Guide to Science Fiction*. New York: Avon, 1979. A brief, positive introduction to Anthony's novels to date. Commments on his inventiveness, complex plot structures, and workmanship as a novelist.

_____. *Reader's Guide to Fantasy*. New York: Avon, 1982. A brief survey of Anthony's fantasy novels to date. "The Magic of Xanth" series noted as a good introduction to fantasy for the science fiction reader, and vice versa.

INDEX

2812-195-A
5-40
C